PSYCH
TRAP

THE HEALING JOURNEY OF PSYCHIATRIC NURSE
WHO WAS ALSO A PSYCHIATRIC PATIENT

Antoinette Kirby, RN

BALBOA.
PRESS
A DIVISION OF HAY HOUSE

Balboa Press books may be ordered through booksellers or by contacting:

Balboa Press
A Division of Hay House
1663 Liberty Drive
Bloomington, IN 47403
www.balboapress.com
1 (877) 407-4847

Because of the dynamic nature of the Internet, any web addresses or links contained in this book may have changed since publication and may no longer be valid. The views expressed in this work are solely those of the author and do not necessarily reflect the views of the publisher, and the publisher hereby disclaims any responsibility for them.

I have published this book under a pen name. All other names of physicians, psychologists, therapists, nurses, hospitals and patients have been given pseudo names to protect their anonymity and confidentiality. No actual clinical scenario has been revealed as my examples are composite characters with details changed. I have not revealed the true location of my work as a psychiatric nurse. My parents are both deceased. Any similarities to personal experiences of others is a coincidence.

Any people depicted in stock imagery provided by Thinkstock are models, and such images are being used for illustrative purposes only. Certain stock imagery © Thinkstock.

Print information available on the last page.

ISBN: 978-1-5043-3059-6 (sc)
ISBN: 978-1-5043-3060-2 (hc)
ISBN: 978-1-5043-3058-9 (e)

Library of Congress Control Number: 2015904786

Balboa Press rev. date: 5/12/2015

DEDICATION

To my two brothers whose love and support never wane.
To Joe. You know who you are. Thank you for unlocking the door.

To My Nurse Colleagues

Some of you know my story. Most of you have not heard it all. In telling it, I in no way want to demean what we do for a living. We chose to be nurses because we wanted to make a difference. The nurse can be the light in the dark place where so many of our patients go. We always wanted to help and make a healing happen for all. It is not our fault that sometimes we did not do the right thing. We do what we are trained to do. We also often do not have the freedom to do what we want because we work under supervision and physician orders. Even in the midst of madness, the nurse can come through with compassion and empathy to touch someone in a way that no one else can. I have only love and respect for my colleagues. We can also be the ones to make a difference by educating ourselves with the truth and stand up for what we believe and know to be true. I apologize for keeping secrets. I have no doubt that some of you may even doubt my truth and think that perhaps you can now explain why I may have sometimes appeared a bit crazy. All I have to say about that is: **If only you could see me now!**

My name is Toni and this is the story about my life as a registered nurse who was once a patient. The good news is that I am well and happy as I reach the end of my middle years. It is my hope that my story will be confirming to others that there is always hope that one can get better, to survive, to heal, and get through most any kind of emotional distress we experience as human beings. I have come to believe after a lifetime of observation, research and experience that Western Medicine is completely off track when it comes to the field of psychiatry. It is a mistake to pathologize life. When we "disease" it, we fall into the "Psych Trap".

I once thought of writing about my life as a psychiatric nurse. At other times, I thought I should write about being a patient. To be honest with myself, I must write with them intertwined because these two compartments of my life were never really separate.

My career as an inpatient psychiatric nurse came to an end in 2006, after a brief medical leave for grief and depression after the death of my father. He had lived with me for five years prior to his death and I was suffering from exhaustion after helping him die of cancer for the previous two years. I think my resignation, however, had actually been in the works for quite some time.

My last year as a psychiatric nurse (inpatient) was difficult. It was not just the exhausting elder care for my mother that I had inherited after my father passed away, as it was conflict with the work I was doing. It became clear one night when our staff psychiatrist asked my opinion on the condition of an adolescent boy in the psychiatric unit where I worked full time in a semi-rural hospital. The doctor, whom normally never asked a nurse's opinion on anything, asked me if I agreed with him that the boy had bipolar disorder, a type of mental illness. Immediately disagreeing, I explained that the boy had been severely beaten up by his mother's boyfriend and that his anger was understandable. I inquired why he thought this to be so. The doctor explained that his mother reported that her son had a rather healthy appetite one night the week before and had played football with some friends. His mother reported that this was not usual behavior and the doctor concluded that this was evidence of a manic state. I voiced my opinion that perhaps the kid had logical reasons to be angry and that a healthy appetite and playing sports were rather normal behavior. The doctor still prescribed several psychotropic medications for the young man, including anti-psychotic medications even though there had been no observed, reported, or documented signs of psychosis. I did not even really observe symptoms of depression. He was angry at his mother because she kept going out of town on trips with the man who had beaten him. The young patient informed me that night that he felt rejected and that he wanted to live with his father so his mother could be with her boyfriend. Later that night, as I was passing bedtime medications, I found myself standing at the medication station with an antipsychotic drug in my hand and having a lot of difficulty giving it to a boy who did not need it. My nursing license was telling me that I had to administer it.

I probably had suffered melancholy moods off and on most of my life. My volatile relationship with my mother was the root of it. I remember feeling sad as early as eight years old. Looking back on my childhood, I would now describe my childhood symptoms to have been rather minor from a clinical standpoint. Many of us simply do not have the easiest time growing up. As I grew up, my mild melancholia subsided as I went to college and started my young adulthood. I was always able to maintain employment and always had many friends in my life. But after the death of my beloved father, I was crashing on a whole new level. I left my job as an inpatient psychiatric nurse in a state of acute grief and depression with knowledge that I was really unable to work. After a brief medical leave, I resigned my position as registered nurse in the psychiatric department where I worked. I was physically, spiritually, and emotionally exhausted. At the same time, I was beginning to spin into a career crisis. Little did I know, that I was about to embark on a six year journey of discovery. It would have to get a whole lot worse before enough insight could be reached to enable myself to move on.

Chapter 1

Psychoanalysis Begins

I now refer to my personal experience with the psychiatric system, as a patient, as chapter one and chapter two. Chapter one was an eight year psychoanalytical process that went very awry. Chapter two, my escape hatch from chapter one, was a twenty year nightmare with misdiagnoses, misguided therapy processes that could not repair the damage from chapter one, and side effects to medications that nearly cost me my life before it was all over.

I began my own experience with the psychiatric system at the age of twenty five when I entered the psychotherapeutic process of psychoanalysis. I was experiencing some symptoms of depression for a number of reasons. I had graduated college with a degree in music and my lifelong dreams of being a professional musician were dashed when I was unable to find the resources for expensive graduate studies. I went to nursing school instead. After graduating, I returned to my hometown of Memphis, Tennessee to find a job. After working for a couple of years for a group of orthopedists, symptoms of depression became apparent in that my life seemed to be going nowhere. My college friends were getting married and I wanted that as well. I had no suitors and thought there must be something wrong with me. I entered into psychotherapy for the symptoms of depression and to find out why I was unable to find the normal experiences that young adults seek.

After breaking down at work one day, I called my mother to come and get me. She was sympathetic to my distress and talked me into going back to work. I did, and she contacted a family relative who was a psychotherapist to inquire about the best way to help me. It was her opinion that a psychoanalyst would be the most qualified of therapists because they had gone through their own analysis and were therefore, able to help others with better insightfulness. I did not know what psychoanalysis was, but I made an appointment with a doctor with these credentials in my city. He also was an MD with a specialty in psychiatry. Psychoanalysis is no longer the most common treatment for emotional distress. However, this process is alive and thriving in America to this day. There are chapters of the Psychoanalytical Society all over the United States and in Europe as well.

My first appointment with a psychiatrist made me very nervous. No one in my family had ever seen one before and this made me feel that I must have a serious problem. I do not recall ever actually asking for the process of psychoanalysis, but wanted a doctor who knew what he was doing. My first appointment was on a Saturday. The doctor, who I will refer to as Dr. Howe for anonymity, was young, appearing to be in his early thirties. He had only been in practice for a few years and was finishing up his own psychoanalytical training by commuting to another city on a regular basis.

Dr. Howe called me in from the waiting room and pointed to a chair. He was in another chair and said absolutely nothing to me at all. *No hello, I thought? Could he at least ask me what I was needing?* He just looked at me in silence, waiting for me to make the first statement. This felt uncomfortable from the beginning. I was still shy, nervous about seeing a psychiatrist, and was desperately thinking that I wish this guy would help me out a little. I was terrified. I could not get a word out. After about twenty minutes of silence, he finally asked what he could do for me. Nervously, I explained that I had been a little depressed most of my life, but had been significantly more so in recent months. I explained that I was unable to finish my music studies, wanted a boyfriend and was too shy to know how to go about finding that. My job was stressful and my relationship with my mother was fraught with conflict. I had been living at home for over a year after moving back to Memphis after college, while renting my own apartment the whole time. I had been too depressed to actually move in and be by myself at that time.

Dr. Howe listened intently. He reiterated that I had symptoms of depression, career problems, and an inability to have normal relationships with the opposite sex. I also had "family of origin" issues that needed to be sorted out so I could finish emancipating myself from my family to be an adult. He stated that I needed full psychoanalysis four days a week and it would be a three to five year commitment. His fee exceeded my whole monthly income as an office nurse to eight orthopedists. He explained that the next time I came in, I would lie on a couch and I would be unable to see him during the therapy. He explained the process of "free association" and touched on the phenomenon of "transference" as the mechanisms that facilitate enlightenment into my past. This in turn, would unleash all of my unconscious obstacles that were handicapping me in moving toward a fulfilled life. This would enable me to change the way I related to the world and thus, giving me the skills to move forward. He gave me hope in that he said I could be treated and still succeed in realizing all of my hopes and dreams. I left his office with thoughts that I must be really disturbed to need treatment four days a week! I later learned that he had diagnosed me with "neurotic depression". Not wanting to share anything about my therapy with my parents, I immediately moved into my apartment on the other side of town.

I began my analysis the following week with four sessions arranged weekly. Dr. Howe accommodated my work schedule by setting appointments prior to work. I was nervous going in that first day because I knew that I would be expected to lie on the couch. This was an immediate discomfort for me because I was unable to see the doctor. I knew that this was how classical Freudian psychoanalysis was done, but the couch made me feel that I was no longer in a partnership for my healing. The couch placed me on uneven ground and it felt submissive, surrendering and I felt like I was not quite in control. I struggled with this for months before I could go in and lie down. It *never* was comfortable. Payment for this expensive process was funded by my parents for about two thirds of the cost and I took on a second job on weekends doing private duty nursing to supplement my job with the orthopedists to pay for the other third.

My next obstacle during those early sessions was the twenty minutes of silence that proceeded each session. As he had done during our first meeting, each session on the couch began with my inability to initiate the session on my own. Waiting for the patient to begin with some free association was also part of the psychoanalytical process. I just did not know how to begin. I was still wanting direction or advice on how to proceed with my life. I did not have a clue yet, what this was about. I bought books on psychoanalysis and began to educate myself on the process.

Instead of beginning with the problems of my life, we began discussing my problems with the couch and with *silence* in general. I was uncomfortable that Dr. Howe never helped me get started. All I needed was a "hello". I wanted him to smile and ask me how I was. He never said *anything*. Those first twenty minutes seemed like an eternity. I was *never* able to begin on my own. After twenty minutes (a dollar a minute back then) time would be running down and he would ask "what are you thinking"? We ended up talking a lot in the beginning about my issues with the couch and the silence. Why was I uncomfortable with these? Dr. Howe explained that everything about my life, my thoughts, my fears, my feelings were material for analysis. It seemed that we spent an awful lot of time analyzing my fears of couches and silence when neither one was a problem outside of the analytical room. It soon became clear that there would be no privacy in my life. Absolutely everything about my life was material for this process.

I remained committed to the process. I did enough reading about psychoanalysis to convince myself that this was a chance for a successful life. Not coming to a resolution of all of my neuroses would equate to failing Life, I thought. I believed that I had to have a successful end someday to this process. I would then be full of enlightenment and possess every skill I needed to implement my hopes and dreams. My analyst seemed to enjoy his job, often stating that because women in his practice were seen four days a week that he saw them more often than their husbands did. He repeated this statement numerous times. It sounded almost like a boast. I also learned quickly the dreaded words that he would say every session that "time is up". After twenty minutes of silence, I felt like I had wasted time and money and just as I got going with it "time was up". For weeks, I left frustrated in that I had made no progress in the issues with my life. It seemed like we struggled for months with lying down and my discomfort with the silence at the beginning of each session. These two issues were the beginning themes of my therapy. Every day, I went in with the expectation of gaining insight into how to make positive changes in my life. Instead, I left frustrated, wondering why couches and silence had become new hang ups and obstacles that I needed to overcome. What did silence mean to me? Why was I uncomfortable with it? Was silence another way to communicate or feel something? Was I afraid of something in the midst of silence and what was that about? There were times when I simply did not have anything to say because we had not even touched on the things that were depressing me. The silence would go on for the whole session on those days, with absolutely nothing said, no words muttered by either of us, no problems solved, and then I would hear "time is up".

My intolerance of the couch and silence finally moved Dr. Howe to try a sitting up method face to face for a while. He finally was able to see that I would never find comfort in that arrangement and we decided to continue four days a week, but sit in chairs where I could see him. I then started to talk. I needed to see his face and know that he was there and present for me. He explained that now the process was a more modified version of psychoanalysis. It was important to eventually get back to the couch, so he could take on a more anonymous role for me to work out my conflicts with others, past and present, through the mechanism of "transference".

As I began to talk, some movement began to happen. We were then able to discuss my childhood, my relationship with my mother, my father, my employers, with men whom I had dated. I thought we were beginning to make progress in at least discussing where my problems were coming from. Psychoanalysis focuses a lot on the family of origin issues with absolutely everything that I could remember. He informed me that analysis, through transference, was to help me relive all of my upsets and traumas and with insight of cause, would come enlightenment and positive change. I bought it hook line and sinker. By this time, I had already read a great deal about this process.

Another relative, the sister of the one who recommended this process was very encouraging that I was engaging in this process. She also stated that the fun part of it all would be what she referred to as the "erotic transference", describing the common phenomenon of the patient falling in love with her doctor. I had never heard of that one. I resolved right then and there that erotic transference, whatever that was, would not happen in my analysis. After all, he was a married man and I did not find him particularly attractive in that way.

Chapter 2

Guilt was a big topic. My mother had done a very good job on my sex education in that premarital relationships were not OK. Dr. Howe once stated that sex "is what adults do". My late blossoming was not normal in my doctor's opinion. These discussions made me so fearful of what my conflicts were about, that I finally went out with a cousin, hung out in a bar, and we went home with two men. Of course, this was material for my analysis as well. The unfolding of my sexuality was discussed in detail with my analyst. It felt rather creepy to me and I did not think this part of my new adulthood needed to be discussed in such detail. However, I had gotten over a hurdle and I began to date.

As I entered into the second year of my psychoanalysis, I was finally able to find my first serious relationship. The face to face technique with Dr. Howe worked better for me and I felt that I was gaining insight into my problems. We discussed my "middle child syndrome", every detail of my childhood, compared my relationship with bosses to my relationship with my father, etc. Both of my parents came out as downright ogres in his opinion and he considered myself to have been the family scapegoat. I mustered up the courage to finally enter into my first serious relationship with a man. I went to a dance class and grabbed a partner when it was clear that there were more women than men in the class. We went for a drink after class and this started a romance that lasted a year.

Of course this relationship was also material for analysis. There were actually three of us in this relationship. Two of us were dating and romancing, one was always watching. My dates, my boyfriend, my thoughts, dreams, and my personal and very private life, as usual, were material for analytical exploration. Dr. Howe then felt that it was time to have me lie on the couch again. By this time, I had resigned my job with the orthopedists and was working full time as a private duty nurse on the night shift. Because I could choose my own hours with this kind of work, I took a case Sunday through Thursday that was a long term assignment. This would leave my afternoons free for analysis and my Friday and Saturday nights open for my boyfriend. I was having more fun at this time, but began to resent that I really did not have any privacy inside my own head. Being my first romance, it became clear that I also did not have any privacy in my own bed.

Because my life was beginning to mature, Dr. Howe talked me into going back to the couch. I had as much difficulty with the couch this time as I did in the beginning, but was aware that it had taken on a whole new discomfort. Now, I was revealing intimate details in my life while lying down and this never felt OK. I guess I was feeling somewhat exposed. Absolutely every intimate detail had to be revealed. That was part of the process. Still committed to the process, I continued on with it all because at least now, part of my problems were improving. I was falling in love for the first time with a very nice man who was returning my affections. I really did not want Dr. Howe to be any part of it.

Because finding a mate was the primary reason I entered therapy in the first place, I mentioned once that perhaps it was time to terminate psychoanalysis. I went in one day, sitting up on the couch and looked at Dr. Howe. I explained that we had some success with all of this. I was dating and was happier and whatever happened, I have better life skills. I explained that it would be alright if my first boyfriend would not be my last. I now knew how to meet others and form relationships. Dr. Howe responded that I was not ready to terminate. First of all, terminating analysis was a process in itself and simply does not end abruptly. Secondly, he stated that I had not worked through my conflicts with men, sex, and relationships because I had not gone through the "erotic transference" that took place in every successful psychoanalytical experience. *Oh no! There was that term that someone had mentioned a year before.* Erotic transference is a Freudian term to explain the phenomenon where the patient falls in love with the doctor, either symbolically, or in reality, and thus giving the analyst and analysand the opportunity to experience the feelings and work on the conflicts through "transference". This is why the analyst sits out of sight. It opens the door for fantasy, perhaps the ripest material for analysis of all.

Chapter 3

"Time is Up"

Remembering that I had been told that I was actually taking a course in "Life", I continued on with all of the discomforts of the psychoanalytical process. I had read in my research in many places that the phenomenon of erotic transference was a common occurrence in analysis, but I simply did not understand it. It was never explained to me and I felt like the whole thing was my doctor's *own* insertion of what I needed to do in my therapy. I made a conscious decision that I would just skip that part because it was *he* that was insisting on it. I would NOT have feelings for my doctor, whom I knew was a married man. I did not understand that erotic transference was not actually real because he informed me that it was partly real, but also partly transference. I did not understand. I avoided all conversation that would lead me down that path of exploration. Dr. Howe had stated that not everyone has this type of transference, but the successful analysis would include this. I did not agree, and started really backing off from my analyst.

I spoke to a friend who had been through psychoanalysis. She stated that she had gone through an erotic attachment to her doctor and enjoyed the whole process, gaining insight and enlightenment into her relationship with others. She claimed that it did not interfere in her marriage. I still did not understand.

My relationship with my boyfriend came to an end in about a year after he told me that he had been seeing another the whole time we had been together.

With my new found confidence, I put myself out there to meet men in new places. But something awful happened. I was date raped. Because I knew the man, I did not recognize what had really happened until a number of years later while watching a talk show on the television that was covering this experience. I realized that had happened to me.

I told my doctor about my experience with a very forward man and explained that I was unable to handle him. He had been known by my family for many years and had actually dated my sister in junior high school. I met him while poll watching during a presidential election. I went out with him, but explained that I had a recent breakup and was not ready to be close to anyone. He indicated that he understood. We planned a dinner and a movie. That would be it. But after dinner, he took me to his place where a hot tub and wine glasses were waiting on his terrace. I could not fight him off and tried to run. It got awful. I became frightened as his eyes appeared to glaze over as if he was no longer present with me. He frightened me. He had forced himself on me and I forced myself away and ran toward the phone to call transportation home. He beat me to the wall and ripped out the phone cords so I could not call for help. Because I knew him, and because he was laughing, I really did not recognize it for what it was. It was a game to him. He finally gave up and drove me home.

As I explained how awful the date was, Dr. Howe then asked "Did you *really* think he was going to take you to a movie?" "Yes", I answered. That was a typical date at the time. Then he asked "What were you wearing?" That question felt creepy, like I had been asking for it all. He expressed the opinion that if a woman dressed in a sexy manner that she may be actually wanting to be assaulted. He stated that when women end up in these situations, that they were unconsciously seeking the experience. He made it sound like it was all my fault for trusting him.

He asked "You *let* him buy you a glass of wine?" I ran from this man once when I ran into him in public, narrowly escaping an encounter. For six months after that night, I would receive many obscene phone calls in the middle of the night. I knew it was him, but he denied it.

When I told the doctor, it was material for analysis. "How did that make *you feel?*" he would ask. That question also felt creepy. "What exactly did he say?" He never expressed concern for my safety. The doctor appeared more interested in hearing the creepy comments I heard in the middle of the night with the phone calls I was receiving. Looking back on it, I was in a bit of danger and never once did Dr. Howe say that his behavior was inappropriate. Dr. Howe made it sound like I wanted all of this and never once told me to call the police. I did not call the police because I could not prove the calls were from him. After all, he had convinced me that this was my fault. I perceived my doctor to just simply believe that I was uncomfortable with men. That is what these discussions made me believe. Not long after that, I came home from a night shift and discovered that someone had pried out my peephole from my apartment door. It appeared as if an ice pick was used, giving my stalker full view of my dressing in my underwear while getting ready for work at two o'clock in the afternoon. This time, I did call the police. They watched my door for a couple of days and that was the end of it.

As I forged on, a new man came into my life. This time, I thought I had found my match. I was ecstatic. For the first time in my life, I was falling in love. We were dating for over a year, when I again went into my therapist's office and announced that I was ready to terminate therapy. I again was told that I was not ready. Then he said something that would alter my life forever.

"You know that the affection you are demonstrating for your boyfriend is actually a displaced expression for your erotic attachment to *me*, your analyst. We need to get through this".

Well, I guess this changed everything. I no longer had any privacy in my own head or with my boyfriend. Determined not to have an erotic transference attachment with my analyst, I had to shut off not only my fantasy thoughts about my boyfriend, but I had to shut out my boyfriend as well. I became very depressed, much worse than I ever felt prior to entering treatment in the first place. I was now afraid to think of anything. I was afraid to think at all. I had been so programmed to have romantic feelings for my doctor, that I became afraid that I would actually have those thoughts. This would be intolerable. When I had a real man in my life making me happy, why was that not a success? My real life was outside of Dr. Howe's office, not *in* it. What was wrong with just going with that? From then on, I gave myself no more opportunities to have romance in my life. Somehow, I still considered myself in treatment for depression. I was depressed, so I kept going four days a week. We were now getting into about four years.

Now, I had no relationship, the desire for such, being the reason I started therapy in the first place. I began seeking other opinions with other psychiatrists. I needed to know if this really was a normal part of therapy. I asked them if I was avoiding something important or was there a possibility that I was in some very bad therapy to begin with. I still did not want to fail my course in Life. I must pass it to find some happiness in my life. The other part of me wanted to flee because this was all beginning to feel sort of sick.

I decided to see a woman psychiatrist. I asked right out if erotic transference was part of a successful psychotherapeutic experience or was I in a terrible alliance with a very narcissistic doctor? She informed me that she would not offer me an opinion until I sever the relationship. This was disheartening, because it was advice about whether I should do that was why I made an appointment with her in the first place.

I soon learned that getting a second opinion on psychotherapy was not going to be like getting a second opinion for surgery. The second doctor I saw was another male. I asked the same question to him that I had asked the last one. This psychiatrist made me very uncomfortable. I had placed a large band aid on my wrist under my watch because I had developed a rash from metal allergy. The band aid kept me from scratching it. As a nurse, I always wore a watch. The doctor asked what was under the watch. Had I hurt myself? Of course not, "do you want to see the rash"? "Had I been cutting on myself?" *No, never heard of that.* By the end of that session, it was discovered that I had made an appointment with a friend of Dr. Howe's.

I told Dr. Howe that I had seen his friend. They apparently knew each other so well that they were on nickname familiarity. I told him about the question of the allergy rash on my wrist. This got analyzed as an unconscious substitute for sexual frustration as a masturbatory exercise. *What?* I was allergic to my watch. That is all. It itched and I scratched it. That *had* to *mean* something according to an analyst. We spent several sessions analyzing why I scratched my wrist in my sleep. It cleared up after a dermatologist gave me a steroid cream. The dermatologist diagnosed it as a metal allergy.

With no relationships and experiencing discomfort with my analysis, I was getting antagonistic around anything that was remotely sexual in content to discuss. The whole process became centered in the analytical room. At least before, I had real life to discuss. Dr. Howe explained that now that I am no longer in a relationship, it was a good opportunity to explore my conflicts about sex and men with *him* through analyzing my attachment to him. We could start by exploring ways to stimulate a fantasy, so I could go back to him and analyze it. He was instructing me, I thought, to fantasize about him to create material for analysis. I remember discussions about what color of underwear I wore. He actually asked about that. He asked if I masturbated. I never could talk to him about such things. I had shut it all down. He wanted to know if I would have my legs open or closed. That would have been material for analysis if I could have brought myself to do it. I remember that conversation with his questioning giving me creepy chills down my spine. I felt violated without touching. At this point, I perceived the doctor to be rambling about his own sexual fantasies as he preceded to tell me that women who do it with their legs open are more open to their sexuality. The closed legged woman would then be closed off to her sexuality. I did not know why he was even discussing this with me. I had not given him any material to analyze around this .All of this was so intrusive that I had practically become asexual by this time to avoid such conversation. He explained that it was important to realize that reality was only preceded by fantasy. He was therefore very big on masturbation to stimulate fantasy. I refused to furnish any material around this for his exploration. We started having sessions again in complete silence. Then the dreaded words, "time is up". Another day gone, another dollar wasted, and another night was waiting for me to get through with all of that anxiety. Sometimes I thought I was going to die of anxiety and depression before he would ever help me with my feelings. I still hoped every day when I went in to see the doctor that I would receive some instruction on how to relieve my depression. But every day I left frustrated and more depressed than when I entered the room. My depression was getting serious.

I began to feel hopeless in passing my course in Life, and disclosed that for the first time, I had thoughts of ending my life. Dr. Howe stated that suicide was the "ultimate resistance to psychoanalysis". *What?* I had to question the validity of a treatment that would drive a patient to suicide. *How could that possibly be helpful? How could that even be an acceptable risk factor to a psychotherapeutic process?* Now, I really was in a clinical depression. It was a cold response, completely releasing the doctor of any responsibility of his part in causing emotional distress with bad therapeutic techniques.

Next, I consulted another female psychologist. I thought that I would see someone that was not an MD. She also declined to give me an opinion about my current psychoanalysis, but offered to work with me if I severed my therapy with Dr. Howe. It seemed that no one would give me an honest opinion. I actually had three sessions with her to try it out. She had no knowledge whatsoever about psychoanalysis. I did not want another sick psychoanalyst. I did want someone who had studied the process enough to understand where mine went wrong so I could move on from it. My agenda had become about healing from this nightmare. She could not relate to my experience. I needed someone to understand how wrong all of this is feeling. The female psychologist simply wanted to start completely over with my childhood, a topic I had grown quite weary of discussing. She did not understand why my analysis felt intrusive. I did not go back after a few sessions. At the same time, I had read a lot of literature supporting the psychoanalytical process with all of the theories of Dr. Sigmund Freud, who invented this process decades prior.

I remember one session where even I was participating in the humor at first. We discussed the theory of a musician friend of mine who claimed that musicians tend to choose instruments that appeared to be similar in shape to the opposite sex. All musicians love their instruments, but I never really sexualized it. Cellos are feminine in shape for instance, so the player may be a bit masculine. This kind of talk may be funny at parties among friends, but my doctor had to take it further. I was a harpist. I had to spread my knees a bit to rest the body of the harp across my chest. Then there was a six foot phallic symbol rising up between my knees. *Even I* had never thought of my harp in that way. My doctor stated that how even playing music could simply a masturbatory exercise. Dr. Howe had actually Freudianized my harp playing and made my music all about him. I did not play the harp for twenty five years. He took that away from me as well.

Psychoanalysts are very big on dreams. Freud was so big on dreams that he wrote a whole book about it. It is a well-known work called <u>The Interpretation of Dreams</u>. Dr. Howe loved to talk about my dreams. Freud maintained they were keys to the unconsciousness. They were keys to conflicts. My dreams had to be revealed because I still believed I had to pass this course. By now I was keeping lots of secrets and not telling him about every little thought I had.

I was still not able to find anyone to confirm that all of this might be going down the wrong road. Apparently, all of the psychiatrists in my city belonged to the same club. If they did not do the same kind of therapy, they at least supported each other in whatever the other was doing. I had heard that they even had a Saturday morning club to discuss cases.

I was beginning to feel rather desperate to feel better. I did not want to be depressed. It had begun to take over my life because I could not get anyone to validate that this was all wrong, nor find anyone who would give me a different approach. I then asked for medication. I was now hopelessly depressed and could find no validation anywhere from anyone. I had learned in nursing school that depression could be treated with medication and I thought this was worth a try. It was standard medical practice and my nursing training supported this thought. Dr. Howe was not against the idea of medication, but declined to be the administrator of it. A psychoanalyst was supposed to be somewhat detached as a caregiver to leave the door open for transference. Dr. Howe could not write me a prescription because it would then define him as having a concrete role as physician. He then sent me to another psychiatrist for the prescription.

I was sent to Dr. Lindenoak (name changed) and was given a prescription for the tricyclic antidepressant, Ludiomil. I had been complaining for a long time that I was unable to sleep. I think I was afraid to sleep. I did not want to dream. I was afraid of what I might dream. I was afraid of what I either had to reveal, or feel guilty for not revealing it. Now I had two psychiatrists and my finances were quite stretched by this. This started a credit card burden that would not end for the next thirty years as I continued to try to get help for what I now know is post traumatic stress.

I took advantage of the appointments with Dr. Lindenoak to ask about erotic transference. I asked why Dr. Howe was insisting on it. I asked if this was necessary to cure my depression. I asked if he would see me instead. I was more comfortable with a psychiatrist who was not an analyst and he appeared to be trying to help. He did say, though, that I needed to go back to Dr. Howe and work out this conflict. I did not know at the time, that when a doctor refers to another that there is an unwritten contract to stay in alliance with each other.

Ludiomil did help me sleep, but it had side effects. This was the first of many psychotropic medications that I would eventually end up taking. Neither doctor seemed to recognize that the drug had side effects. I got no relief from my anxiety or depression and the dose kept getting upped to hopefully increase its effectiveness. The opposite happened.

On Ludiomil, I started walking in my sleep. We analyzed the sleepwalking to be anxiety about unresolved conflicts. I started to eat in my sleep. I was gaining weight. We analyzed that to be my unconscious attempts to cover up my sexuality. *Why was I afraid of my sexuality?* Because I was afraid of working out my transference attachment to Dr. Howe. Later, in my inpatient nursing work, I had patients that related similar experiences with this type of medication.

Dr. Howe knew that I liked movies. He asked me one day who my favorite actors were. I named off about four handsome actors as my favorites. I told him who my favorite actors were, all popular in the eighties. He then said to me, "hmmmm, I am not sure I really look like any of them. Often patients will be attracted to certain actors because they look like him". That would be "transference". I thought that to be rather egotistical to have even brought the subject up.

Another side effect of tricyclics in the higher doses is carbohydrate cravings. I could not get enough carbohydrates. The cravings were so strong, that I would wake up in the mornings only to find empty cereal boxes on the floor with no memory of eating them. The weight gain made me more depressed and anxious. Before I had ever heard of eating disorders or bulimia, I developed a full blown case of it. I remember waking up in the kitchen in the middle of the night once while eating an ice cream sandwich. It is amazing what one can do while sleep walking. I began to booby trap my kitchen by placing heavy tape across the entrance, thinking I would awake and catch myself doing it. That did not work. I did not sleepwalk apparently when I had been expecting it. I stopped stocking any "ready to eat" foods in my apartment. I stopped purchasing cereals and crackers that could be eaten out of a box. I only had unprepared foods in my apartment to stop myself from eating anything carbohydrate laden. This worked. But then, I started to sleepwalk in other ways. I woke up several times and found my key on the outside of the door. I still have no idea what I was doing. The anticholinergic side effects gave me dry mouth that felt like cotton. This was a side effect I could not tolerate, but was the only one that was actually recognized as a side effect by the two doctors. I remember one morning, I found the trash sack in the refrigerator and the milk in the pantry. I was apparently quite busy in my sleep.

At this time, I had left nursing altogether and was working as a sales representative selling first aid supplies. My nursing background was an asset on this job and I beat out three hundred and fifty applicants for the job. I had a route and drove a first aid truck around my assigned territory. I was behind the wheel all day. The tricyclic antidepressant interfered with my mental processing. I would always leave my therapy sessions in a state of anxiety and the Ludiomil slowed down my ability to process incoming information. I was unsafe behind the wheel. I had three near misses for serious accidents. Once I ended up in someone's yard and could not remember how I got there. I had never had these thing happen before taking the Ludiomil. Another near miss took me across four lanes of oncoming traffic and I ended up heading for a crash write into a business building. I was screaming while trying to break and the truck stopped, barely missing a head on collision with a concrete sign in front of the building. I had never even had a wreck in my life when all of these things were happening. It was only while on a tricyclic antidepressant. I thought that something bigger than I must be watching out for me to have narrowly missed such a potential disaster.

As the eating disorder took over my life, I finally was able to tell Dr. Howe about it and begged him to help me stop it. We terminated with Dr. Lindenoak, and he sent me to his office mate and colleague, a female psychiatrist who had a thick European accent. She was about the sixth psychiatrist I had seen by then. She hinted that maybe there was something wrong that was causing my depression, never even entertaining the idea that perhaps the side effects to Ludiomil were making me worse. She prescribed a new antidepressant, a monoamineoxidase inhibitor, called Nardil. This antidepressant would need to be accompanied by a special diet and it could be dangerous if not followed. No aged products, like cheddar cheese or smoked meats. No alcohol, except a certain kind of wine. No anesthesia's or antihistamines. Consuming these products could be lethal. I could not tolerate this medication either. The bulimia did stop and the carbohydrate craving stopped (both unrecognized at the time as side effects), but it did nothing for sleep and depression. I felt a buzz in my head and simply could not tolerate it. Around this time, I developed a lot of gastrointestinal discomfort that led me to see a gastroenterologist. He wanted to do diagnostic testing with an endoscopic procedure. Because I was on a monoamineoxidase inhibitor, I could not have the sedation that would be required. It could have been lethal. I went back to Dr. Howe and we agreed to discontinue the MOI medications. I was developing gall bladder disease, most likely due to chronic dieting and purging, obvious side effects to tricyclic antidepressants.

Dr. Howe finally, after, six years, gave me a prescription that he said would help. The drug was amitriptyline, also known as Elavil. He did not explain to me that this drug could have side effects as well. It was also in the tricyclic family of drugs. I had already proven to be unable to tolerate this type of drug.

Eating disorders were going through a rage at that time and Elavil was beginning to be common treatment for sufferers of anorexia because it actually was known to cause weight gain. Why my doctor gave me this drug for complaints of weight gain, is not something I understand. I gained more weight and became more depressed. The dose kept getting raised. The anxiety and sleep eating returned, and thus the panic and purging.

I know as a nurse, that amitriptyline has made a comeback for chronic pain, especially neuropathic pain. The dose for that can be as little as 25mg. For depression around 1983, my dose for depression eventually reached 350 mg nightly. I was a complete mess. But I slept well on that medication. I had to take it two hours before I went to bed. I then had to go to bed or I would spend the night wherever I was. Like Ludiomil, Elavil had anticholinergic side effects that made emptying my bladder a strain. All in all, I took tricyclics for about five years and the constant straining to empty my bladder led to surgery for a bladder suspension at the early age of forty one. This procedure is common only in women who have had the bladder strain in childbirth. I had never had a child. There is no other explanation for needing this surgery except for the side effects of tricyclics.

The chronic dieting, purging, eating, sent me to an early cholecystectomy (gall bladder surgery). In the hospital, I stopped the Elavil. At the same time, the carbohydrate cravings stopped, the sleepwalking stopped, the sleep eating stopped, the rapid weight gain stopped, the eating disorder disappeared and never returned again. This was the beginning of the end of my analysis after eight years. While home recovering from abdominal surgery, the doctor I saw four days a week for eight years did not even call to see if I was alright. He did not care about his patients. I had decided that he was only interested in processes that would feed his own ego. He was a narcissist from head to toe who liked to have affairs with women in their heads. I was done.

Chapter 4

A New Approach, "It is Drugs You Need"

While recovering from surgery, I decided to go back to school. I had been working in a pediatric ward in a county hospital when nursing began to change. My nursing experience up to this point had been under the licensure of a vocational nurse. With changes coming, it became clear that I either needed to go back to school for an RN degree or leave nursing altogether. Because I had a degree in music, I elected to go to graduate school for a Master's degree in rehabilitation counseling, rather than to spend three years getting a second bachelor's. I finally fired Dr. Howe and began my studies at the state university that had a campus in Memphis. I left my analysis, feeling that it was incomplete and a failure. I had at least by this time begun to blame the failure on the analyst, not myself. The way psychiatrists covered for each other, knowing that one may be harming a patient was inexcusable. Nurses are trained to report each other's errors and it was not unusual for us to write incident reports on each other. Physicians, from what I could observe, did not report each other's errors very often. Now I had been given more baggage than I began with. I was in a sense "giving up". I reconciled my previous dreams of having my own family and decided that I could at least have a satisfying career and do some good in the world.

As I adjusted to life with weeks without four doctor appointments in it, my emotional distress did not resolve. I still felt that my thoughts were not my own. Fear of transference attachment continued and blocking out these thoughts was difficult. I avoiding dating altogether. Lying on the couch for eight years had been like a trance, a hypnosis, maybe unconscious programming. Because my course in "Life" had failed, depression began to set in again. Six months would pass without seeing a doctor of any kind. No medications were taken during this time. My thoughts were my worst enemy. After seeing a doctor four days a week for eight years, it was like a very bad divorce. Everything was left unresolved. The issues haunted me daily and my insomnia persisted. Wanting desperately to be rid of this influence in my life, I was still living in fear of thinking, dreaming, feeling, or even expecting to ever be OK. After all, I had failed therapy, my only hope of a normal life. Several years prior to ending my analysis, I had inherited a little money from a family farm sale and had let my parents off the hook in funding my treatment. I only had enough left to get through one year without working and begin school. I had wasted my inheritance on futile psychotherapy that gave no significant results in reshaping my life. Thinking backward, it was clear that I was better off before the whole process began. All of that therapy and all of those drugs and their side effects because a young lady wanted help in finding romance.

I liked graduate school, but could not shake off the unresolved issues of my therapy. I was still single, now unemployed, my future uncertain, and I had all sorts of emotional baggage that I never had prior to beginning therapy. My insomnia drove me to try another doctor. Perhaps now that I was no longer in treatment, someone would help me. My new doctor came recommended by my general practitioner. He was housed in an office connected to another well-known hospital in my city. I will refer to him as Dr. Taylor (a name change).

My first appointment with Dr. Taylor was different than the others. This doctor actually spoke to me from the beginning, making me feel comfortable in his presence. He acted like a real physician, performing a physical assessment with heart and lung sounds and a measure of my blood pressure. I informed him of my psychoanalysis and how it ended. I felt this was contributing to my depressive symptoms because I had developed so much fear with my own thoughts. The only way to keep Dr. Howe out of my life was to keep him out of my *thoughts*. Because my thoughts had belonged to him for so long, I lived in fear and anxiety all of the time. I told Dr. Taylor everything. He listened intently and expressed sympathy and understanding. He took a thorough family history. He also explained to me that psychiatry had gained new insights into the cause of mood problems and that it was now theorized that most emotional problems were organic in nature. Theories of genetically inherited mood disorders were becoming more commonplace in modern medicine.

During my second session, Dr. Taylor stated that he thought I had manic depression. To overcome the stigma of mental illness around this diagnosis, the medical profession had recently renamed this syndrome to be bipolar disorder. Dr. Taylor based his diagnosis on the fact that I had a relative that had emotional problems after World War II. I had always been told that he suffered from "shell shock" in the service and he was never the same after coming home. Perhaps I have something in common with *him*. His other criteria for my diagnosis were the severe side effects that included atypical behavior while I took tricyclic antidepressants. His theory, along with others, had begun to use the response to the tricyclics as a diagnostic tool to define bipolar disorder. Virtually the whole medical profession used the side effects to a medication to be evidence of a mood disorder. I could not recall ever having been manic, though I had a period after college when, for a brief time, I had become a Quaker. Though the Quaker religion is a peaceful way of being, this did not work for me for many reasons. I had simply viewed this part of my life to be that place between music school and nursing school, as a time of self-exploration. It was a growing up time to figure out who I was, what I wanted, and how could I do some good in the world. Dr. Taylor interpreted this to mean that possibly I had been manic and this was also criteria to earn me the diagnosis. Looking back on this theory, it does not make any sense at all. Quakerism is a peaceful religion, not crazy at all. Always socially activistic, they had run the Underground Railroad for slaves in the Civil War. They are good people. Even though it did not quite fit me, I still have a lot of respect for these peaceful people.

Feeling a bit stunned, I stated that Dr. Howe would never agree. He had diagnosed me with *neurotic depression*. The doctor then stated "well, the march of science must go on" I thought this physician had guts. He had the courage to make his own opinion, his own assessment and make his own diagnosis. I had to go with this. It gave me hope. Dr. Taylor stated that it was a shame that I had gone through all of that therapy. What I *really* needed was medication for a *physical* illness that could be treated. He informed me that this was good news. I could have a normal life with the right medications. I had hope for the first time in a long time.

Having a diagnosis was a relief. This was my escape from the mental prison of psychoanalysis and feeling like a failure. I had been misdiagnosed and medication would fix everything. As my graduate studies began to take off, hope was present within me for the first time in years. There would be no therapy, just medication management. I would see the doctor only weekly until I was stabilized on medication. The first medication prescribed was another tricyclic called Nortryptiline because Dr. Taylor said that it did not cause hypomanic symptoms, the term he used for my side effects to the others in this category of medications.

The Nortryptiline also had side effects. I quickly became restless and a bit irritable. I still could not sleep. He diagnosed my irritability, though my behavior was normal, as hypomanic symptoms secondary to a tricyclic." Hypomania" is a term that means "less than manic, but a bit speeded up". It is not a state of true mania. Hypomania is not pleasant, whereas true mania is absolute euphoric. I had never had euphoria. We abruptly stopped the Nortryptiline and I was prescribed Lithium Carbonate.

Lithium was the most common treatment for manic depression (I prefer this term over bipolar disorder). The United States started prescribing it around 1970. It had been approved in Australia much earlier, as the doctor explained it's origin. Dr. Taylor explained that it was not actually a drug, but a type of salt. It was well tolerated, he informed me, and stated that people who do not have manic depression get no benefits from it at all. We tried it for about a month.

Dr. Taylor was mistaken. The lithium, was worse than the others. I felt absolutely intoxicated on it. This drug required weekly blood draws for drug levels to measure a predetermined "therapeutic level". I could not get dehydrated or I would become toxic. There was a fine line between therapeutic levels and drug toxicity. Being out in the sun too long was no longer a choice. My side effects began before any therapeutic effects could be achieved. Graduate school was going well and mental impairment could not be tolerated. *Hey, where is the normal life I was informed about?* I still could not sleep. I had the constant feeling of being in a tunnel with a ring in my ears. It felt similar to the effects of the nitrous oxide I had experienced with dental work.

Because blood levels for the lithium were not reaching therapeutic levels without intolerable side effects, this medication was discontinued after only a few weeks. I continued to go to school with a ring in my ears. This never really completely resolved.

Next, we decided to address my sleep, thinking that would be helpful. He recommended high doses of Tryptophan at night to promote rest. The second night, I awoke in the middle of the night with severe stomach cramps. When reported to Dr. Taylor, he stated that this was a known side effect and he took me off that "over the counter" nutritional supplement.

Next, we tried Halcion for sleep, a rather new medication at that time (but still available today). Halcion was one of the quickest intolerances I would ever develop in my whole experience with medications. The day after the second dose, I developed a *louder* ring in my ears, a buzz in my head and it did not work very well for the sleep. My hearing felt impaired and there was a feeling of pressure in my head. This reaction frightened me because these side effects lasted about seven weeks. I had only taken two pills in total of this drug. I was afraid that it would not resolve. I began praying a lot that I would be OK. I prayed to God in the middle of the night. I prayed for healing. I prayed to my grandmother to help me. Now, I actually *wanted* silence. The loud buzz in my head kept me from sleeping or even resting. I was scared. This impairment interfered with school. My concentration was impaired. My hearing loss was significant. I thought I was ruined for good. Seven weeks was a long time to put up with this, but it slowly resolved. Unfortunately, to this day, there is a ring in my ears. There is no memory of this prior to taking these drugs with Dr. Taylor.

Yet, Dr. Taylor was kind. I began reading the books that were now popular on the "New Biopsychiatry". I was still so relieved to be free of Dr. Howe, that I continued to work with Dr. Taylor to find the right medication for my new diagnosis. There still was hope.

Next came the drug, Trazadone, also known as Desyrel. This one would actually help me sleep. Drowsiness set in about 20 minutes after it was taken. After several years of poor sleep, this was a relief. With improved sleep, I began to feel better for the first time in many years. Dr. Taylor felt that this was the only medication that I would need. We saw each other less frequently and I was able to finish my first semester of graduate school with one A and one B for grades. I felt like I had been to hell and back in a brief four month period.

I loved my studies. My degree was training me to work with people with disabilities. Now *I* have a disability. I could be helpful to others in a whole new way on a professional level. My life's work would now be about helping others to live normal lives, like me. A person with a mental illness.

At the end of my first semester, my school announced that it was restructuring the degree program and it would cease to exist for the next two years. My choice was to wait two years to get on with my life or transfer. Feeling a need to escape my life in Texas and all of the misery of the last eight years, I moved to a Midwestern state far from Texas and transferred my credits.

Leaving my home state and family was hard. Females in my family had not been encouraged to be so adventurous and independent. My decision was met with resistance from my parents. I wanted to move on, find a new life with new people. Dr. Taylor supported me and said it might be good to move where no one had a "book on me". I told myself that I was OK now. Others did not need to know about any of this. I was finally getting better. Due to the emotional abuse of my analysis, I resolved to never marry or even try again. I would get a graduate degree, find a career, and make a difference in the world. Damaged goods, I thought, but still capable of at least a satisfying career. I was now thirty five years old. Eight months after terminating my psychoanalysis, I visited Dr. Howe on my way out of town. I informed him of my new diagnosis and my new medication. I asked him why he had not seen it. Why was he more of a philosopher than a physician? He did not have much to say. We both knew that this was a final goodbye. At least I had confronted him a little. Dr. Howe said very little to me in that visit. He actually had tears in his eyes, but deprived me of resolution by not acknowledging that it all could have gone a different way. I am not a litigious person, but desperately wanted closure. I still owed him $600 dollars. I informed him that I would not be paying it, nor for the visit that day. He replied "I do not expect you to". That was the first hint in the whole eight years that the man might have some humanity. I left his office thinking "good riddance".

Chapter 5

I moved to a Midwestern state and began graduate studies at a state university for my Master of Arts degree in rehabilitation counseling. This degree can be defined as training in psychology with a focus of working with individuals with disabilities, both mental and physical. Future career goals were not yet defined with my degree. The choices were many. Shortly after I arrived to town, the need for medication follow along soon became apparent. I made an appointment with a new psychiatrist in my new home town. He had been recommended to me through a referral service. I will refer to him as Dr. Wilson, not his real name.

My history of psychoanalysis was of no relevance to consult a new doctor for only medication management. I never wanted to rehash that story again. Dr. Wilson was informed of my diagnosis and my good state of stability. I simply asked for a prescription. I had a poor impression of Dr. Wilson from the beginning. He seemed extraordinarily eccentric and he wore very thick glasses. He did not really interview me. As he proceeded to fill out insurance papers with questions, I again explained that I had the cash to fund my visits with him. He then spent an hour and a half filling out insurance information that would not be filed. I received a bill for a double session. Feeling uncomfortable with this physician, I cancelled my next appointment because I did not feel that he heard anything I said. Dr. Wilson actually called me back and insisted to know why I had cancelled. Trying to be polite, I lied, and informed him that my general practitioner would be monitoring my medications. Of course, there was no general practitioner at that time.

Dr. Wilson stated on the phone that this was inappropriate and that I should come back to seem him. Feeling a little harassed, I was confident that the right decision had been made to stay away from him. It was almost like he was a bit desperate for a patient.

Needing someone to continue my prescription, I consulted the local chapter of the National Alliance of the Mentally Ill. This is a local support group that is rumored to receive funding from the pharmaceutical companies (I discovered that fact years later). After a meeting, I met a woman about my age who shared with me the name of her physician, who actually *was* a general practitioner. He managed her medications. I made an appointment with him right away because my medication was getting low in count.

I liked Dr. Sutton right away. He could treat everything as a general physician. Dr. Sutton did the admission physicals at the nearby psychiatric hospital and knew about psychiatric medications. He was confident in his skill. He was a good listener and my story was revealed to him. He did not believe in psychoanalysis and described it to be a "dinosaur" in treatment. He was a believer in the theories of biopsychiatry. He had even published a few papers on it. He confirmed me that I had been misdiagnosed and that my psychoanalysis had gone very wrong at the hands of an inept doctor. My general healthcare was also placed in his hands. I felt safe and comfortable with this physician.

Dr. Sutton was *not* comfortable with the fact that I only took one medication. In spite of the fact that I was doing better on *only* that, he felt that I should try Lithium Carbonate again. He made this conclusion without any symptoms of any kind apparent. Following his advice, it was tried and the same side effects as the year before quickly emerged. I walked in without an appointment and stated that I felt intoxicated out of my mind on this stuff and we agreed to stop it. I simply could not tolerate Lithium at all. I also saw no need for it.

Shortly after, the "new" SSRI antidepressant, Prozac, arrived on the market. He added this to my regimen because of continuing complaints of anxiety. I continued in school, doing well in the academics, but still had threads of anxiety and haunted dreams of the past. Prozac became quickly popular. *Everyone* appeared to feel better on Prozac *at first*. I would take Prozac for the next ten years. That was not all, however. Afraid that I would somehow flip up into a mania (I still had never had any mania), he added Tegretol to the Trazadone. Tegretol was an anticonvulsant medication, given for the "off label" (meaning not FDA approved for that purpose) use to combat the manic side of manic depression. Dr. Sutton also informed me that the drug studies had shown that some Prozac users actually *lost* weight. That made me happy after the forty pounds that I had gained on tricyclic antidepressants. It would be another decade before the truth came out about weight issues and SSRI antidepressants. It has been documented that over time, the average Prozac user could gain up to sixty pounds! I was one of those.

As I continued with school, the Tegretol made me drowsy. Trazadone caused a morning fuzziness and made it difficult to wake up. A small price to pay, I thought, for staying stable. I had learned that none of these psychotropic medications come "free". Somewhere, before I graduated, Ativan was added "as needed" for my "free floating" anxiety. Now I am on four psychotropic medications: Trazadone for sleep, Prozac for depression, Tegretol to prevent the mania that had never been experienced, and Ativan for anxiety.

In spite of it all, I functioned fairly well until I got to the end of my program and the stress of writing a thesis was quite high. I was required to complete Comprehension Examinations that included "orals" where I had to defend my answers verbally to a staff of faculty. All of us were normally stressed. Because I was secretly a psychiatric patient, I was compliant with my medications. I took Ativan prior to my comp exams. Somehow, I made it through them and graduated with a straight A from this institution. My internship was to begin with the state Division of Vocational Services, a government agency that exists in every state in America. Here is where my life as a professional and my life as a patient merge for the first time.

Chapter 6

I Am a Professional Counselor

I would hone my craft as a rehabilitation counselor during my internship. There was a caseload that needed attention due to a staff vacancy. This is where I started working with clients on a one to one basis. I had my own office with administrative support. My job was to assist individuals with disabilities to find and maintain suitable employment. My agency could provide education, sometimes even college, "on the job trainings", career counseling, adjustment to disability counseling and direct assistance in finding a job. I taught career seeking skills and did mock interviews. The paperwork was typical of any government agency, quite copious. I was happy with this work and was often recognized with a number of certificates and awards for achievement.

I did not disclose to anyone that I had a diagnosis of my own during my internship. When another vacancy opened up in the office, it was clear that my supervisor needed to make a hire. The State at that time had a moratorium on hiring due to some funding problems. Because we were low on our "token disabled" as employees, I was able to get hired by disclosing that I had a disability. My supervisor was surprised to learn that my disability was a mental health diagnosis. He admitted that if he had known, he would not have made the offer. Because I had proven myself, he hired me.

My career as a rehabilitation counselor went well for many years. I struggled with medications and their side effects. I would undergo a number of changes through the years, always throwing me off balance for a while. In spite of it all, I maintained and excelled at my job. My caseload was changed to give me the mental health referrals. My caseload of about one hundred clients was about fifty percent of chronically mentally ill individuals referred to us from the County Mental Health Center. The majority of these clients had become chronic and severely disabled to life and employment. They were part of a system that included government disability benefits. I was appointed to be the liaison with the County Mental Health system and became quite familiar with its many therapists, case managers, and psychiatrists. I became their advocate. I would later be honored at an awards banquet for community contributions for my work as a liaison of Rehabilitation Services and the County Mental Health Center.

I learned what the more chronically disabled individual looks like. I learned of their struggles to maintain stability, stay out of hospitals and I learned of their medications which were much more difficult than mine. In some cases, I shared the *same* medications, but was quite aware that I had never needed to be in a public system or a hospital. I still had *never* had a manic episode, but shared the same prescriptions as those who had. Still, I was doing well. It still felt much better to need medications than to deal with the warped pressures of my psychoanalysis. I would rather be on medications than lying on a couch with the intrusions of my thoughts.

Some of the clients of County, also did not look that sick to me. Some were on so many medications that employment was a tall order. I became an advocate for people with mental illnesses. I attended meetings, sent many to school with success, and turned a relatively low success caseload into a successful one. I had many individuals who returned to work while living with diagnoses and medications. I believed in them. If I could do it, I believed that others could as well. I loved the people I worked with and believed in them. After all, I was one of them. I would stay at this government job for twelve years.

My job had its pressures. There were mountains of paperwork, deadlines to keep, statistical expectations for case closures (meaning return to work for the client) and I got as stressed at times as my coworkers. Looking back on it all, I simply do not see that I ever became any more or less stressed than anyone else. Because I had an illness, I got in the habit of complaining to my doctor that I was not handling things. We always attributed the least little upset as pathology, we would add or make a medication change. I had become to believe that normal stress of living were somehow going to affect me worse than others because I had a disability. My physician changed my Tegretol to Depakote. As par for the course, there were side effects. Depakote was another weight gainer and several years after I started it, half of my hair fell out. This was distressing because I had spent a lot of money and effort for about six months to lose the weight with the help of Dr. Sutton through a liquid fast program. Depakote is known as a weight gainer, but I was unaware of this when he started me on it. This is a known side effect. Depakote was another anti seizure medication to combat the episodes of mania that I still had not yet had. They must be working, I thought, I still have not had a true mania. Looking back on it, I have to say I never noticed any therapeutic effect of any anticonvulsant medications at all. Using them for psychiatric reasons had become the mainstay treatment, though they had not been approved by the FDA for this off label use. For me, they were placebos. No effect whatsoever, except making one very obese and drowsy.

I did have anxiety, though. I was successful in suppressing my past traumas with Dr. Howe, but was unable to forget it all. My anxiety was treated by Dr. Sutton and benzodiazepines were always in my purse. I did not realize that during those days, I had become accustomed to medicating just about any feeling that was not blunt. Grief needed medicating. A little joy meant that perhaps I might be escalating and I would medicate that down with a benzo. I was afraid to feel any extremes of emotions, being told it was abnormal. Prozac was constant during these years and I went ten years without crying. The inability to cry was a blunting of my emotions from the medications. Still, I was willing because Dr. Howe was gone.

My career with Rehabilitation Services came to an end after a huge tidal wave of change that motivated a lot of my colleagues to take early retirement or simply leave. If I was going to make a change, it would be back to nursing. At least I had that to fall back on. Several years before I left, I took courses by independent study, took clinical refresher courses, and started to do a little nursing on weekends to catch up. I would soon complete the Registered Nursing degrees that I had begun twenty five years earlier. I passed my exams with flying colors.

After I received my RN license, I resigned my government job and took a position with a free standing psychiatric hospital in a nearby town. I decided that I was weary of being the "token disabled" on the job and decided that I would never disclose this again to anyone. I wanted to be like everyone else and I thought that taking medications did not make me any different. Yet, I still wanted to be of service and enhance the lives who suffered from emotional disturbances.

Chapter 7

Inpatient Services

I was not prepared for my first day at Middleton Hospital (name changed). It also did not take long to question if I had made a mistake by resigning my government job. This facility was uncomfortable from the beginning. We had our share of patients that appeared to be in emotional pain, but of great concern, was the town police department's use of the hospital for dropping off trouble makers in the community. I later learned that it is easier for the police to drop off the community rebel rouser at the psychiatric hospital than it was to do a full police report and an arrest. Those who were hospitalized for genuine emotional distress were housed with the substance abusers, the verbally abusive and sometimes, the criminal element. I wondered when "anger" became a "mental illness "when no violence was involved. Why were public offenders on probation dropped off at the hospital instead of being arrested? Why was an adult sexual perpetrator placed on the same unit as a female who had been abused by such? Why wasn't the perpetrator in jail, instead of a hospital unit? We were an acute and short stay hospital. We were never equipped to handle the criminal element. Most people only stayed inpatient seventy two hours.

Patients at Middleton were not well supervised. We housed about twenty acute level adults, and about twenty adolescents. Their units were separated by a nursing station cleverly constructed with a common door between them. This enabled a nurse to work both units at once.

The hospital also had a detention youth program for adolescent males. They were in a separate locked unit, but the nurses from *my* unit were often called when a "take down" was necessary and a "show of force" was required to get a rebellious youth into isolation. This happened frequently in this facility. Due to previous complaints by the State, this hospital no longer used restraints on patients of any age. There have always been concerns about the safety of leather restraints. The method of six people manually holding a squirming youth on the floor for as long as forty five minutes was not exactly safe either. There were rumors of suffocations and injuries from this method of restraint in other facilities across the country. Other patients were sent to their rooms while the patient was held down long enough to get a calming sedative injected into the gluteal region. The incarcerated youth would then be hand carried by six to eight people to seclusion and the door would be slammed shut. Two to four hours was an average stay in isolation for an adolescent.

The unit down the hall from mine was a program for adjudicated youth males. These occurrences may be expected in a detention youth center. However, not all of these young men were hardened criminals. There were some arsonists, drug dealers and potentially violent young men in this unit. But there was also a milder population mixed in that seemed confused by all of the chaos. A few of these, basically children, had just been caught with a little marijuana or had been convicted of shoplifting, hardly hardened criminals. In a residential center like this one, there was no parenting or love taking place. I suspected that most of them left worse than when they came in. The more innocent youth were in the same unit with the very bad boys and learned from them.

At any given time, there were at least half of the patients on suicide precautions. This meant that their whereabouts and activity had to be documented every fifteen minutes. In this facility, this was a full time job for somebody. I sensed early on that this was not a facility where compassionate care was given. I was instructed to never give too much attention to any one patient because their need for such was described as "attention getting". I did not understand this because it was apparent that one would not *be* in a psychiatric facility if they were not lacking something somewhere in their lives. On my very first day, a woman twisted her socks together and tightened them around her neck. Alerts were called and her actions were intervened by staff. She then had to spend the night in the day room where she would be in the "line of sight" of staff for the next twenty four hours. I wondered if this incident could have been prevented by showing a little compassion with empathic conversation and listening to help her explore her feelings.

Middleton was a "for profit" hospital and admitting as many patients as possible in an evening appeared to be my main job. We turned them in and out so fast that some barely received any attention at all. All admits had to have a nursing assessment by a RN by law. We were admitting so fast, that I was unable to keep up with their names. When the medical doctor came in the day after admission for their physical exams, he would ask me where patients were. I was embarrassed that most of the time, I did not even know their names. There were sometimes forty patients and most of them were only in the hospital a few days or less. I simply could not keep up with them. Management kept us short staffed for profit over safety. There were only two to three nurses for thirty to forty patients with two to three psychiatric technicians on staff to do the safety checks, help with showers, and conduct the therapeutic groups.

A psychiatric unit is a milieu setting, meaning that patients mingled in the day room, ate together and attended groups up to six times a day. The day room was not big enough for such a large number of patients to be adequately attended to. I worried about the safety of such a mix of patients in a small space. This unit was simply not organized or supervised to the degree that it should have been. During my brief eleven months at this hospital, I witnessed a few minor assaults and a patient threw a radio into the back of a physician. These incidences began to occur more frequently when a new neuroleptic medication was marketed to us as the new antipsychotic to be used for acute episodes of psychosis. It was Geodon. Always ready to try something new, physicians used quickly on our unit. I did not observe it to be used for the patients who appeared to be in an actual state of psychosis. It seemed to be given for the ones who were irritated by their involuntary incarceration in a psych unit. They used antipsychotic medications to calm people down. One physician informed me he was not particularly impressed by it efficacy. They all kept using it because plenty of free samples were always provided to hospitals at the beginning of the drug company's marketing a new drug. Compassionate care simply did *not* exist in this facility. Safety was in question, not only for my patients, but for myself *and* my license.

Take downs were a common occurrence in the adult unit as well. Again, the community rebel rousers were mixed in with the emotionally distressed. Because of the poor staffing patterns, the local police were often called to help with the take downs. Even though other trained personnel would answer the emergency call, the unit relied heavily on the community police. A uniformed policeman only added to the shame and guilt of the "take down "experience, leaving the patient to feel that they had committed a crime. The ambience of the milieu, for those who were genuinely in distress, found themselves in a unit where the police presence added a sense of shame to their acute distresses. Seclusion policies, dictated by law, were to be used only in cases of threat to harm oneself or others. I saw it used for other purposes on numerous occasions.

I was still asking when anger became a mental illness. When did disturbing the peace become a mental illness? When did drug dealing and using cocaine become a mental illness? When did voicing a desire to kill someone become a mental illness instead of cause for a night in jail? I became a psychiatric nurse because I wanted to give compassionate care to those who had suffered. I wanted to show kindness and give healing to the spirit in their hearts. I wanted to make a difference. In this facility, I felt like a warden.

Early in my employment at Middleton, I came across a familiar face in the crowd of patients. Kevin, (name changed and now deceased),had been my client about seven years earlier with Rehabilitation Services. He had presented a disability of arthritis that was interfering with his ability to perform his job as a maintenance worker. He was in his late forties when he came to me and had twenty years behind him on his government job at the local university. Kevin needed a more sedentary position. While planning his rehabilitation plan, Kevin disclosed that he carried a lot of sadness around with him because his mother had shot herself in the head in front of him when he was only seventeen years old. He commented in our session "my mother did not love me enough to stay around". Being the well-meaning counselor that I thought I was, I offered him some counseling around this. He expressed interest and on government funding saw a psychiatrist as part of his rehabilitation program. I arranged and authorized his treatment with a local psychiatrist. The psychiatrist placed him on antidepressant medication and gave him some counseling. We were successful in finding Kevin more suitable employment and his case was closed soon after.

I was then surprised to see one of my favorite rehabilitation clients in my unit as a psychiatric patient. Keven remembered me right away when I reintroduced myself, now seven years later. Kevin stated "it is all over, Toni". "They did electroshock therapy on me and I have had brain damage. I cannot think most of the time" Later that night, I looked at his chart and discovered that he now carried a diagnosis of Bipolar Disorder. How sad, I thought. We did not know that years ago. This would not be the last time that Kevin would appear on my path as a psychiatric nurse.

Electroshock treatment was performed at Middleton on weekdays. A typical treatment would be three times a weeks for three consecutive weeks. Because I worked the evening shift, I only saw the after effects of treatment. Evening headaches were common. Over time, I had many complaints of memory loss, both short term and remote. I do not recall anyone raving about success after their shock treatments. It appeared that only females had asked for it. I do remember one male patient who was a teacher in the public school system in a nearby county. He did not look particularly ill, but was anxious about his past. He revealed to me that he had made a grave mistake by having an affair outside of his marriage. He was full of guilt and regret because this destroyed his marriage and he lost custody of his three children. Devastated by his own actions, he came into the hospital asking for ECT. His request was granted. He was hoping to calm his anxiety down enough to be able to live with himself after what he had done. He did not carry any mental illness diagnosis except anxiety, which was I understood. He was hoping to numb himself out from the uncomfortable feelings he had brought on himself.

On another occasion, I began speaking to a patient who was staying close to the nurse's station. He informed me that he had just been let out of prison after eight years. I asked why he had been in prison and he calmly replied, "murder". Trying not to act shocked, I asked what brought him to the hospital. He then said, "homicidal ideation". Again trying to hold my composure, I asked who he felt like harming. He replied, "anybody". I watched him closely that evening. How did our assessment department miss adequately screening this man to approve of him being admitted on our unit? Why would a convicted killer be loose on a unit with women who had been abused and needed a feeling of safety? He did not otherwise appear ill. When our psychiatric triage department accepted this patient from another hospital emergency room where there were no beds, this detail had not been disclosed. This was common around the area hospitals. My state had a severe shortage of psychiatric beds and admissions happened wherever the emergency departments could find an opening. The truth was often not disclosed because the emergency rooms needed a place to dump the patient. Many admissions were ambulanced to us from far away towns and occasionally over state lines. Again, I asked, "jail cell"? I called the administrator on call to inform of this admission. I was instructed to just "keep an eye on him". It is a public offense to use "fighting words". How could one night in a hospital possibly keep the community safe from this person? This patient was one of the very few patients that did NOT receive medication during his stay. The year is now 2000.

Patients getting through the assessment department was a constant challenge. We never knew who was being admitted until they arrived from the hospital who was trying to pass the patient on to somebody else. I remember a news report in a nearby town that a patient with a history of murder has escaped a psychiatric hospital and had not been found by the local police. The uproar in the community was loud and covered in the news. The question was asked how a murderer could have been allowed to escape. I was more concerned why the murderer was in a hospital to begin with instead of jail. Crime is not a mental illness in my opinion. There are state run facilities to house convicted criminals who were deemed to be "insane" I could not understand why they were in an acute stay hospital. The game the triage workers played to dump their troubled patient's on other facilities made it very easy to understand how a murderer could be in a community hospital. The community police were never involved with these assessments in the emergency departments. It was not their job, apparently.

The criminal element also used the psychiatric department to their benefit. On one particular weekend a "suicidal" patient was admitted on our unit. He had been addicted to illegally obtained opiates and he claimed to the ER doctor that he wanted off the drugs and out of the lifestyle he was leading. He was admitted late in the night.

The next morning, the patient asked me for an opiate pain reliever. I explained that he was on an opiate protocol for withdrawal and I would not be allowed to administer him that drug. He looked surprised and stated that he did NOT come to the hospital to get off the drugs. He had no intention to get off the medication that he had been purchasing on the streets. He admitted to me that he also was a distributor of the drug on the streets. I inquired why he made the claim the night before in the ER that he was suicidal and wanted off drugs. I also asked him if he was still feeling suicidal. He stated he was NOT suicidal and that he wanted a pain pill. I asked him what he was doing at our hospital.

The patient proceeded to inform me that he was there to hide from his drug dealer. Apparently, his mother was in business with them. They had been moving from one motel to another for weeks to hide from a drug dealer that the patient owed $2000. He stated that if the dealer found him he would be killed because he did not have the money. I explained to him that this scenario did not meet hospital criteria for being an inpatient. His mother then came in to the unit to visit him. Unaware what her son had just told me, she asked how long her son could stay inpatient. "He is very suicidal, you know", she said to me. I asked both of them to a meeting room to ascertain what was going on. They both admitted to running from a dealer who had threatened to kill my patient. I inquired if his whereabouts were known to the dealer. The mother said "yes, he calls me daily to find out if he is still in the hospital". It was unclear if they were friends with the dealer or were genuinely afraid of him. I pointed out to them that we had a video camera outside of the locked door and asked for a description of the dealer, so nobody would mistakenly let him in. The mother told me that he was about six feet tall, wore pin striped silk suits and always had a diamond necklace of a large cross around his neck. She also said that he was Hispanic, gave me his name, and stated his hair was in a long pony tail. The son then said "Shhh, Mom, do not give her that much information!" The patient denied being suicidal. He did not want off drugs. I explained that no hospital criteria was met here and that the unit was not a place to hide from the criminal element. The mother expressed concern that if we discharged him, he would be wacked when he walked outside the door.

I took the situation to the medical director of the psychiatric unit. I explained the dilemma we were in that the patient was in danger of getting wacked if discharged, but that there was no justification for a hospital stay. Of greater concern, in my eyes, was that I had the name, location, and description of a drug dealer in our community that had probably committed murder. The psychiatrist laughed at me. I wanted to call the police. She instructed me not to. She said that the police would only laugh at my dramatic story and not act on it. It would also violate my patient's rights to confidentiality, even though the man was clearly not even ill. Still concerned that my patient could be in danger, I contacted the social worker and again related the story. He stated that the patient made his own bed and if he gets wacked outside our doors, it would be because he had asked for it. The situation was of no concern of ours. The drug dealing patient attended the same groups as the adolescents and others who were trying to get off their substances. I wondered how therapeutic our groups were with such a mixed population.

The adolescent program averaged about twenty patients at any given time. We admitted age thirteen and up. Many of our patients were students of the nearby high school in this small town. Self mutilation, the act of making cuts on oneself was a common occurrence in this hospital. Though we had adults, men and women, engage in this injurious act, it was most commonly seen among young adolescent girls. Psychiatrists had a belief system that the majority of females that engaged in self mutilation has been sexually abused at some point in their life. I did not assess that this was always the case. On one occasion I witnessed a young adolescent female explaining to another that if she made a cut on her forearm, that she could get away from her parents for a weekend by getting admitted to the hospital. The youths were actually training each other how to do this. Hospital admissions for adolescents does not require parental permission or involvement. The act of self mutilation was seen as a serious symptom of deep disturbance and most of these females were diagnosed with a personality disorder. However, I also saw that it could be used as a manipulative game with the adolescent getting a lot of attention, as well as a diagnosis. It did appear to be an addictive habit in some patients. They would claim that it was the only thing that could relieve intense emotional pain and anxiety. We nurses speculated that it might actually induce an endorphin rush to relieve anxiety. There were a few cases that required skin graft repair because the scar tissue was too damaged to heal. Most self mutilators would choose the same spot over and over. Even though patients were searched for contraband upon admissions, it seemed like mirrors and sharp objects had a way of getting in the unit. I often thought that if I were the parent of a teen, a psychiatric hospital would be a very unsafe place to get help.

Chapter 8

Time to Move On

As I continued my work at Middleton Behavioral Hospital, it became clear that I would soon be making a job change. Patients simply were not well supervised and the truly distressed were not receiving compassionate care. Escapes were commonplace in this facility. Even while on safety precautions, patients were allowed outdoors on an hourly basis to smoke. It was not unusual for a patient to hop the fence and leave. It would not take much planning to see that this would be easy if one could jump high enough. I also witnessed a couple of patients giving another a lift to make it over the fence. If they were on a seventy two hour "mental health hold", the police could be called to enlist their assistance in locating and bringing the patient back to the hospital. Finding the escaped patient was never a priority with the community police in this rather small town. This was usually not pursued and the doctor would simply discontinue the hold and the chart was signed out to be "left against medical advice". The patients who escaped were generally the community rebel rousers that were brought in by the police to begin with. The generally distressed patient wanted help and were unlikely to even try.

The issues around the "seventy two hour hold" presented problems in itself. It appeared necessary for those who were intent on harming themselves. They needed a place to stay for a few days to diffuse these feelings. Just as often, it was used for the physician's convenience. A doctor taking call would have to come into the hospital after hours to see a patient who wanted to voluntarily check themselves out. This inconvenience was often circumvented by the admitting doctor routinely placing *all* evening admissions on a mental health hold. This would legally prevent any voluntary check outs of the hospital. Sometimes it took a lot of courage for an emotionally distressed individual to ask for help with an admission. The automatic involuntary "hold" that was slapped on them was another source of humiliation and shame around their condition. Some patients informed me that they would never ask for hospitalization assistance again if their free choice about doing so was taken away. I surmised that many people in need would never ask for help again, even if they needed it. Mental health holds were filed with the legal system and thus a harmless individual could end up with a legal record as well.

Another issue with the seventy two hour mental health hold was with those patients who used it to their advantage. This group does *not* include the genuinely distressed and ill patient who generally saw a need for hospitalization. Others found that if they show up in any emergency room, claiming to be suicidal, they could get admitted to the hospital and receive a place to stay and food to eat for three days. These professional patients used the system to their advantage. Homeless people sometimes would claim suicidal ideation because they needed a place to stay. Somehow, I understood this distress. Usually uninsured, however, this is a contributing financial factor as to why psychiatric units have been closing by the dozens across the country. Staff would fondly refer to these admissions as "three hots and a cot" stays in the hospital. If one knew how to work this system, a patient could literally travel across the country with little or no financing. Staff referred to these admissions as "travelers" because they were recognized as having been seen a year before on their migrant path. Patients were literally discharged back to the streets in these cases when their mental health hold had expired. It was my observation that there *were* also truly ill individuals that learned to survive this way without any family support, jobs, or places to call their own. There are, no doubt, thousands of people who live this way because they have no place to live. Discharge plans always included referrals for outside services, but without resources or a roof over their head, follow up often did not occur. There were no follow up services in this hospital to investigate if the discharge plan was ever utilized.

One very busy week, patients were admitted and discharged so rapidly that there were three "completed" suicides in patients known to have been discharged that very week. After witnessing a patient assaulting another, I decided that I had enough of this environment and resigned my job. My nursing license was not safe there. I lived with the fear of a sentinel event due to poor supervision. I still believed in giving the distressed patient empathic treatment and care. It could not be delivered here where all my time was taken up with endless admission assessments at the expense of good supervision and therapeutic support for my patients. I lasted only eleven months at this facility. Several years after I left Middleton, I heard rumors that there had been a completed suicide on the unit and a nurse had been seriously injured while trying to prevent an escape. I knew that I had made the right decision. I accepted a position in another psychiatric department that was connected to a general hospital in another nearby town.

My new position was in a full service general hospital with its own psychiatric department attached. Memorial Hospital had a small psychiatric department that, like Middleton, was a locked unit. Due to physician shortages for inpatient psychiatric services, we were only able to take up to ten patients. We averaged about seven patients at a time. Memorial was better staffed than Middleton with two to three staff for seven patients. I was only responsible for two to three patients at a time. Of course, supervision of the full unit was a department responsibility. Memorial was a much kinder place with caring nurses and better attention given to patients in distress. We had a small recreation room with a treadmill and we utilized therapies in art, music and movement. Therapeutic groups were of higher quality. We did not have a formal adolescent program, but still admitted youths from age fourteen and up being housed on the same small unit as the adults. The adolescents attended the same groups as the adults. I viewed my nurse colleagues as compassionate and caring for the welfare of others.

Unlike Middleton, where "one to one" attention was discouraged, I was expected to give individual attention to all patients on every shift. I always felt privileged to be able to speak with a patient for an hour every day to give therapeutic conversation and encouragement. Overall, I felt that Memorial was a much better place to stay in times of need. I worked full time on the evening shift.

I was able to perform my job well, I thought, and never disclosed to anyone that I carried a serious diagnosis of my own. I wanted to be like everyone else and not be known as having any medical differences. I had been seeing a new psychiatrist for a couple of years at this point for my medication management. My family practitioner had referred me to a friend of his because he thought all of my medication would be handled better by a psychiatrist. I reluctantly went to him, having not seen a psychiatrist for almost ten years. Dr. Noonan was a kinder psychiatrist than I had ever known. He was always encouraging, upbeat, empathic and positive. I saw him every three months for prescription refills. Over time, my story came out with the trauma of my psychoanalysis and my diagnosis. He never pushed me to disclose anything that I did not want to. We did not engage in formal psychotherapeutic processes. Dr. Noonan was simply a supportive doctor who was able to reinforce me with more confidence than the others. I continued on medications and the occasional prescription changes that always brought with it a period of adjustment and new side effects. Overall, I was doing well. Dr. Noonan sometimes referred to me as the "poster child" of manic depression. I lived a clean life, did not drink or do street drugs and was compliant with my medications. As a result, I could live with a mental illness and have a reasonably normal life. Looking backwards, it is easy to see why a model patient can be a "poster child" for successful treatment when there was absolutely no mental illness to begin with. It would take me a few more years to figure that one out.

In spite of it all, I had carried threads of sadness most of my life due to many factors. I accepted this as part of my "biological condition", not recognizing many family and social factors. I learned to live with the memories of my failed psychoanalysis and just accepting myself for the way I was at the time. I was an educated professional that just simply accepted that there were many things in life that were not possible for me to have because of damage that had been done to my psyche by my first psychiatrist. Though I never disclosed the diagnosis to anyone at Memorial, it was discovered one day that a number of the nurses were taking antidepressant medications. I never told them I was taking so much more. By this time, I was taking so many medications that I had to keep them in a large button box from the craft store. A simple "daily reminder" container could not hold them all. Looking back on it, I would have to state that Dr. Noonan treated me on the diagnosis of others without making his own assessment. I still had never had a true manic episode and Dr. Noonan was never presented with one in me. I still consumed anti manic medications for that infamous manic episode that I had not yet had. My parents, getting up in their years, had recently moved in with me. I found a friend and soul mate in my father as we brought music back into our lives. We went on long walks together, took care of my disabled mother, and were having a lot of fun in friendship. The next five years would be among the happiest in my life.

Chapter 9

Memorial Hospital

I was happier at Memorial with a manageable patient load and better staffing patterns. I took the evening shift to give myself time during the day to be with my family. My father brought love and joy back into my life. We filled our free time together taking care of my mother and playing music together. A frustrated musician, himself, we even started to perform a little in public. We were members of the local harmonica club and the local chapter of the American Harp Society. We went to meetings, performances and music conventions. We shared expenses in the household, so I did not have as much pressure to make financial ends meet. Early on, however, I saw things in my work that were beginning to disturb me.

Because of our affiliation with the county mental health center, Memorial admitted more patients with more severe and chronic diagnoses. This population was used to repeated hospitalizations and preferred Memorial over more crowded and noisy units in nearby hospitals. They received more attention here. We had our share of the homeless and the "travelers". We were skilled at medical protocols to withdraw an individual from alcohol or street drugs safely. It was done better at Memorial than at Middleton. Early on, however, I had a sense of restlessness about the way people were diagnosed, admitted to the hospital, and my own secret condition that suddenly did not make sense to me at all.

Manic depression, or better known as bipolar disorder, was the diagnosis of the decade. When I first started my nursing studies, this was considered to be rather rare. In the late seventies and early eighties, eating disorders were the disorders of the time with clinics and hospital programs springing up all over the scene. These units are now rare and in the seven years that I worked in the inpatient setting, I rarely saw this diagnosis. In the decade of the "eighties", it was theorized that depression must be inherited and antidepressant medications became commonplace. The diagnosis of bipolar disorder was no longer rare as side effects to anti-depressants became obvious, especially as the new selective seratonin inhibitor medications, such as Prozac, hit the market. Professionals were not recognizing that agitation, increased depression, or the lack of relief from it, could be side effects to the meds, not a disorder in itself. These symptoms, or side effects in my opinion, were diagnostic to earn one to be diagnosed with bipolar disorder. My own physician was very clear that the response to an antidepressant was a diagnostic tool for more serious conditions. It is a puzzle to me that physicians just did not discontinue a drug that a patient got worse on.

All of the sudden, displaying anger on a psychiatric unit earned a patient the label of "bipolar" disorder. Conflict in a relationship meant that one was either bipolar, personality disordered, or both. Side effects to antidepressant medication were used as a diagnostic tool for bipolar disorder. Almost all adolescents that have rebelled against discipline were diagnosed as bipolar. All relatives of those who already carried the diagnosis, also received it themselves. Victims of sex abuse, or any kind of abuse, were bipolar and "personality disordered". I was confused, feeling like we were placing people in a diagnostic box and never letting them out. It was going against my belief system that people could get well and recover from even the most difficult of experiences. My own diagnosis was placed in doubt. At the same time, I continued seeing Dr. Noonan and taking many medications. Doubt about it all began to set in. I had to question my instincts when the whole profession of medicine was educated, credentialed, and was supposed to know what they were doing. Who was I to go against all of this?

Seclusion and restraints were used much less often at Memorial than at Middleton. They were used on occasion when staff perceived the patient was going to lose control of their behavior, verbally threatened staff or others, or was perceived to be a danger to themselves or others. The perception of staff in defining these occurrences was another matter.

Unlike Middleton, who abandoned the use of leather restraints, Memorial did use them. I attended training on an annual basis how to do this "properly". The patient was usually lowered to the floor with a variety of nonviolent techniques. They were placed on their stomachs and literally "hog tied" with their hands behind their back with their ankles included in the restraints. They were then gently placed on a hard surface to be placed on a gurney (wheeled stretcher) and taken to the isolation room where they were then restrained to a bed that was anchored to the floor. Fortunately, more often than not, a patient would simply be escorted to isolation by staff with security officers behind them, and placed in isolation without the use of restraints. The "show of force" by numbers of personnel was enough to prod a patient to cooperatively go into isolation.

When a patient was admitted in the throes of a psychosis with uncontrolled behavior, was high on steroids or cocaine, or was threatening violence, I could understand this process. Emergency room staff have to use restraints more often than we did as people abusing substances often did present a potential for a violent scenario. This was not the usual case inside the psychiatric unit. More often than not, I had to question why it was used in many cases. Adolescents were placed in restraints more frequently than adults with their rebellious and often angry verbiage. I observed that informing a patient that they would be going to isolation would only escalate their anger and even promote rebellion due to the humiliation of it all. A friend of mine had her leg broken while being placed in restraints at another psychiatric facility. I was never comfortable with isolation and restraints. In the seven years that I worked in the inpatient units, I only initiated isolation one time.

My poor patient came to the hospital in an acute state of a psychosis. He was a middle aged man with no known history of psychosis or mental health treatment. He was beginning to take his clothes off in front of other patients and I knew that I had to get him off the unit. His behavior was not threatening or scary to anyone because the patient was so obviously unaware of his inappropriateness. He made no threatening remarks or advances. He simply was psychotic and was laughing and thought he was acting silly. I called security, as this was protocol, but was able to handle the process of getting him to isolation without a scene or restraints. With security standing behind me, the other staff nurse beside me, I light heartedly asked the man if he would like a private room. He laughed and said "yes". With his clothes half off, we escorted him to isolation and closed the door without any need to restrain him. He was totally cooperative and was singing silly songs as he walked in. He was then observed to be leaning against the wall singing songs with laughter for the next several hours. The patient was given an antipsychotic medication. The physician who was "on call" came in to see him and started a routine dose of anti-psychotic medications to be continued after the isolation was over. He gave him a diagnosis of "psychotic disorder".

Fortunately for this harmless individual, a different physician was on call for the weekend. By morning, his admission laboratory reports had been received on the floor. The doctor on call, stated that the patient did not have a chronic psychotic disorder. He had an electrolyte imbalance that was quickly corrected with a couple of natural supplements. His antipsychotic medication was discontinued, the supplement corrected his electrolyte imbalance, and he quickly returned to normal. Unfortunately, he remembered everything he had done and was tremendously embarrassed. He stayed in the unit for three days and never left his room again during that time. I volunteered every night that week to be his nurse and I brought him his meals to have in his room. In inpatient psychiatry, meals are generally taken together at a dining room table to promote normalcy and routine. I had sympathy for this nice gentleman who could not believe that he had taken his clothes off in front of ladies. It simply was not his normal behavior and in my "one to one" with him, it was clear that he was a gentleman in every since of the word. When we knew that he was clear of psychosis, he was transferred to another medical hospital in an ambulance. As I approached his stretcher to say goodbye, he looked at me with a look of gratefulness in his eyes that I will never forget. It was one of the most touching moments in my work as a nurse to see how grateful he was that he had been spared the humiliation of judgment. He did not need punishment or restraints. He was spared a misdiagnosis and ongoing medications by having the correct assessment with objective laboratory reports. He motioned with his finger to come closer to tell me something. He lightly kissed me on the cheek and said "thank you". I was touched and watched as they transported him to where he belonged, a medical bed.

In his state of unawareness, this patient taught me that things are not always what they appear to be in a psychiatric unit. We need to be careful how we diagnose and there may be many medical reasons why a psychotic episode occurs. Psychosis, clearly can be an altered mental state a mind, not necessarily a chronic condition. Those who become chronic are still a challenge for medical professionals. We still do not have all of the answers.

All of the medical profession, as well as in the patient population need to be aware there is still, as of this writing in 2014, no absolute conclusive evidence of any chronic mental illness that can be found in a DNA marker. It is clear that people can become psychotic, but the etiology of this is still unclear. We still are unable to measure chemicals from the central nervous system and "chemical imbalances" are still hypothetical in origin, not proven fact. We discuss the existence of serotonin, norepinephrine, epinephrine, and dopamine, but it is thought that there may actually be hundreds of neurotransmitter chemicals in our brains. So what are we treating when we further alter chemicals in our brains with medications that have not proven dramatic results in most cases? So far we are unable to objectively measure any of these chemicals. To give a patient antidepressants to increase serotonin production, is speculation at best, at least at this time.

Sometimes we can see a difference in a brain scan, but what does this show? These studies still do not look at the genes and the alleged heredity of such conditions. A difference in a brain scan could indicate brain injury, chemical alterations, birth defect or injury, all of these with capacity to change moods and behavior. I have questioned scans that show new cell growth after medication administration as a possible natural compensatory system to repair itself for the cell damage done by the medications. There is no question, that we have disabled individuals in some sort of neurological impairment. But the etiology of the symptoms is still open for debate and further research is needed. To assume that one psychotic episode is going to be the first of many because of an unproven hypothesis of genetic disease, is very short sighted. At the same time, it must be acknowledged that some have repeated occurrences.

It was my observation in my nineteen years of working directly with chronic mental illness, that the majority of the time, individuals are kept on medications and had repeated episodes. When a diagnosis was given that fell into the categories of major affective disorders (indicating of organic origin), they were rarely given a chance to live without medications that could alter the chemistry in their brains. The sad truth is that this nurse often witnessed these diagnoses being given on an admission page upon entering the hospital because the form that was used, asked for a diagnosis for insurance to approve the stay. This was defined before the patient was even assessed or seen by a psychiatrist. Sometimes an astute physician would change the diagnosis after seeing the patient, but most often the physician rarely changed it. Of equal concern was the practice of a couple of our psychiatrists, to have given pre-signed copies of the 72 hour mental health hold form, leaving the full assessment to a triage worker, Triage workers in emergency rooms are, at least most of the time, done by psychotherapists, who are not medical professionals. The consequences of this were often serious when a medically compromised patient would end up in the psychiatric department when a medical bed was more appropriate. Psychiatric departments are rather sparsely furnished for safety reasons and individuals who needed side rails, call bells with cords, and oxygen assistance were not appropriate in the psychiatric department. More than a few times, emergency services had to be called to attend a psychiatric patient in need of medical services because they had not been medically assessed in the emergency department. This was a dangerous protocol. Emergency room staff, typically are not fond of the psychiatric admissions. They needed to get people in and out as quickly as possible. Psychiatric patients took up a lot of their space and time as they had to wait for the triage worker on call to arrive. Emergency staff were often poorly trained in assessing a psychiatric patient. If we want to continue to medicalize emotional problems, then the patient in distress deserves a full assessment that includes both the mental and the physical condition.

I worked for almost seven years at Memorial. My growing discomfort with the system increased day by day. At this time, my father had been diagnosed with cancer and was entering the last two years of his life. I started to experience grief long before his death. I was losing my soul mate, the sweet loving father who had brought joy, love and music back into my life. At the time of his diagnosis, I knew that his kind of cancer had a very poor prognosis. My father was determined to beat it. After his death, I spiraled downwards to a depth that I had not ever experienced. I knew that I could not work for a while and entered my supervisor's office to resign. I would cash out my retirement account early to fund a leave from working. My supervisor liked me and offered me a disability leave instead to give me time to evaluate my plans. I accepted his offer, knowing full well, that I had no intention of staying in the field of psychiatry.

Chapter 10

A Patient Once Again

My disability benefits required me to be in treatment. A psychiatrist had to document that I was in treatment and was complying with the rules and regulations. By this time, psychiatrists had stopped doing regular psychotherapy as often because the field had become largely pharmaceutically based. American health insurance programs preferred to fund the lesser trained, and more economically affordable, psychotherapist with a Master's degree. I have found that these professionals are often very good at what they do. They are trained in the "talking therapy "approach to healing and are often less likely to recommend medications. An empathic therapist can be worth their weight in gold. However, as in all levels of therapists, it can also go awry. Psychotherapy is not a benign process. It can be either transformational in a positive way, or it can be devastatingly damaging if not done properly. Little did I know that I was about to experience once again, the latter.

The sadness I felt the morning my father passed away was overwhelming. The soul mate friendship we had enjoyed in the past five years of his life had brought me such joy and happiness. My siblings, my mother, and I had stayed up all night in vigil to his passing. He left us after I had fallen asleep with my head on his shoulder while holding his hand. I played my harp at his bedside the night before after he became unconscious. It was October of 2005. His passing was accompanied by the sorrows of Hurricane Katrina playing in the background on the television. By the afternoon, a great sorrow was setting in like I had never known. Memories of the past also began to haunt me. I had successfully suppressed my traumatic past because love had entered my life and once again I had lost it. Love comes in many forms. Not all of us are lucky enough to experience romantic love and all the joy it can bring. But love in any form, from anyone can carry us through life. My psychoanalysis had robbed me of my childbearing years and impaired me to having any romantic relationship in my life. I had accepted that and learned that love in *any* form can be just as joyful. My father had remained totally in love with my mother for sixty seven years. But he also had room in his heart to let me remain his "baby girl" into my middle years. He loved his grandchildren and mentored all of them. I had learned to experience love through my music, through my friendships, and yes, I always remained his baby girl. My sorrow that day took me to the past, realizing that I may never know love again in *any* human form. This compounded my loss.

The beloved relative, a cousin of my father's, who tried to help me when I was a depressed young lady looking for love, by referring me to a psychoanalyst, was unable to attend the funeral. Needing a connection to my father, I visited her on the east coast a month after he passed. I had always adored this cousin even though distant geography kept us from seeing each other most of my life. I was often told by relatives that I was a lot like her and I always took this as a complement. I never blamed her for my bad experience in psychoanalysis. She meant well and it was the doctor that was unskilled at his craft, not necessarily the process of analysis itself. I never told her how it went for me. She had a good experience with this methodology. The theories of Sigmund Freud have remained a source of interest and entertainment to her to this day. When I visited her, she was comforting and caring. She gave me her easy chair in her bedroom every morning and brought me comforting herbal teas. It was only natural that our conversation would turn to the topic of psychoanalysis. As I began to explain it to her, she was absolutely horrified. For the first time *ever,* I began to process this painful experience by revealing the details.

I had sought help with this trauma many times over the years. Other psychiatrists, not trained in the psychoanalytic process, were unable to understand. They used medications instead. I never got my complete story out to any of them. There are details that had never been disclosed to *anyone.* My relative ended up being the one who started me down the road to healing by listening to my story. It became clear that she, and only she, could finally put this to rest. It would take over my life again for another five years.

My relative blamed herself for referring me to the process. She did not, however, refer me to that particular doctor. She was never responsible for any of it. Her psychoanalyst, younger than she, was still practicing in his late seventies. She called him and told him my story. Her doctor was rather famous for authoring the text book on psychoanalysis that was used in many training programs for years. In fact, I recognized his name because there was a copy of this text on the unit in the hospital where I worked. The only doctor that used it, however, was also a physician who crossed boundaries. I had seen him sitting side by side on a female patient's bed while she was rubbing his back. My report to my supervisor about this incident went unaddressed. I was horrified to have witnessed this because I was afraid for my patient that she was being victimized in the same way I had been.

The famous doctor was practicing in New York City. My cousin called him and explained my experience. She was quite upset about it all, feeling like she had played a part in it. He told her that my experience was the worst story of sex abuse without touching, he had ever heard. That was a comforting confirmation that it *really was* awful and impairing. I was able to let go of blaming myself. It would take a few more years before I could actually sew up the wound. There would be further injury before it would be all over. By this time, I had actually become a mental patient. I had all sorts of diagnoses and drugs to support it.

Attempting to follow the rules to earn my disability benefits that could briefly support my leave of absence from work, Dr. Noonan referred me to one of his colleagues in the hospital clinic where I saw him for my medication management appointments. Cindy was a psychologist. Dr. Noonan would adjust my medication and Cindy would do some brief counseling around grief. I told Dr. Noonan that I had no interest in rehashing my past ever again. I only wanted help for the present life transition and grief that I was going through. An even worse nightmare was waiting for me.

Apparently, all therapists of all credentials, seem to be unable to start with a patient at the place where she now resides. They all have to rehash the past. I had inherited the care of my very disabled and demanding mother with my father's passing. This stress, along with my grief, was what I needed help with. I was having a career crisis as well. My mother was rather shaming to me as a child and my issues with her were resurfacing as I became her primary caretaker. Of course, that had to be processed again even though I was now skilled at processing this on my own. I became weary of talking of the past and ended up having conflict with this therapist. It seemed that I was simply unable to ever have any professional help of any kind without traumatizing me with the past. One of her confusing assessments was that I had idealized my relationship with my father. She was critical of this and wanted to have me fault my father for something. She thought I had been unrealistic about this soul mate relationship. I did not understand what possible benefit I would have by trashing my father now, shortly after his death. *Let me have my memories, at least, of the one person that I knew loved me.* A father and daughter often have a special relationship. Why in the world would she find pathology in love? I had enough of processing the past. I could not win or overcome it. I went home and after a spat with a sibling, I overdosed myself with a two month supply of sleeping pills. I would spend the next twenty eight hours at home, alone, in a coma.

Chapter 11

The Worst is Yet to Come

My body metabolized the drugs naturally and I awoke the next evening. I remembered that I had an appointment with Dr. Noonan that afternoon. What I did not know, was I had lost a whole day. I arose from bed and was unable to stand. I fell to the floor. My muscles were too lax to support my body. I did not want anyone to know what I had done, so I was determined to make my appointment. I bumped into the walls, the door frames, and fell to the ground again. I bumped into my bird's cage and it fell to the floor after smashing me on the forehead. It took over an hour to be able to stand up. I showed up at Dr. Noonan's office about thirty hours late. My face was black and blue from the falls. I still thought it was day before. I was disoriented to time. Looking back on it, I do not even know how I made the thirty mile trip to his office. My face was covered in large purple bruises. I had to tell him what had happened.

I still fondly think of Dr. Noonan as one of the good guys, even though I would soon reject all notions of inherited mental illnesses and lost faith in medications that dulled the happy emotions and perpetuated the negative ones. He respected my work as a registered nurse in the psychiatric field and did not want to put a mental health hold on me. He knew how humiliating that would be. I had to promise to stay the night in the hospital or he would have to follow the law and slap me with a hold. For the first time, I was now inpatient in a psychiatric hospital.

At least, it was not the one that I worked in. I was not on a legal mental health hold, but I was hospitalized under coercion and threat of one.

I knew the game of a hospital. One must take their medications and be compliant with the system. This hospital, however, looked like the first one I had worked in, Middleton. I had heard that this hospital was intrusive with their safety searches. They were known to have had two completed suicides on the unit. Even I was afraid of this place. During my safety search, a process that I had done hundreds of times by now, I bent over, spread my cheeks and mooned the two nurses. I knew exactly what I was doing. I had twenty five years of frustration built up inside of me and I was going to pop. I can only imagine what that looked like in the nurse's notes. It was my way of saying "Fuck you!" I had already decided that absolutely everything about this system had no validity. I realized how much better Memorial was at giving mental health care. This place was a pit in the worst proportions. I walked into the hall and saw the words "suicide precautions". I rather laughed at that. I was already over that. Because they were short on beds, I ended up in an acute wing like I had never seen before. They put me in a room with a mattress on the floor and placed a water pitcher beside it. There was no furniture. This was the most humiliating experience of my life and could not tolerate this inhumane treatment. I was no danger to anyone. I certainly knew better than to harm myself in a hospital. *I worked in one, remember?* I was angry. I started to cry a little. I left my room and asked the nurse where group therapy was to be held. She informed me that I would not be allowed to go because I had been crying and this was seen that I was not stable enough. I became furious. I conducted groups in my hospital. How dare she make this erroneous assessment?

My assessment, done by a triage worker in the emergency room never asked me any medical questions. Looking back on it, I believe that recent medicine changes and stresses may have caused impulsiveness that I had never had in spite of everything I had been through. It is clear now. My new therapist had talked Dr. Noonan into changing my medications. She was not a doctor, but seemed to have some influence on this. If I had been properly assessed, it would have been obvious that I had a recent surgery for a shoulder injury that required a general anesthesia. I was coming off the pain pills, had quit Trazadone cold turkey after twenty one years, had the addition of a new drug, Lexapro, and Dr. Noonan had given me a Seroquel for sleep. I had actually been on four different antidepressants at once, including Ritalin, an amphetamine. I had been thrown into a state of akisthesia, the darkest place I had ever been.

My two days as an inpatient was a rude awakening to how awful the field of psychiatry had become. Another way to look at it, was that perhaps we have not made significant progress with these kinds of problems since the sixteenth century. As a psych nurse, I was often reminded by patients of Nurse Wratchett from <u>One Flew Over the Cuckoos Nest.</u> I began to understand their perspective. Anyone could feel like a cuckoo in this environment. I was going to have to prove that I could sleep through the night to be released. They gave me the drug Seroquel for sleep, a drug now known to shorten life spans and cause neurological impairments. Television commercials disclose this freely while advertising the drug. It made me foggy and mentally disorganized. I was quite aware how nuts I was beginning to appear to others. Seroquel interfered with cognitive function. Anyone would appear ill on this drug. The next night, I cheeked it, a trick my patients often tried. I lied and told them I slept well. I faked it all night long. Who could possibly sleep in that environment?

I attended a group session with a psychiatric technician who had very poor therapeutic skills. He encouraged us to enlist as many friends as possible because we were so draining to be around that we would burn any one friend out. *Was this supposed to encourage me?* Now, we are not likeable by anyone. How therapeutic was that? I was furious again. I began to feel like the very thing they treated me as such, a pathetic, unlovable, worthless crazy person who would drain anyone in my life. That evening, I saw the worst "take down" I had ever seen. By now, I thought I had seen it all. But this one horrified me. How could my Dr. Noonan take part in all of this? I was losing faith in him as well.

In the early evening, I was sitting in the day room and overheard a conversation between a social worker and a patient. There was no threatening behavior or anything appearing to be out of control. The patient was simply refusing medications, which was his legal right to do so. The social worker gave him a choice to either take his medications, or be placed in isolation. "What?" I thought. This was a clear misuse of isolation procedures because there was no threat to anyone. He simply refused his meds. Then all hell broke loose. The community police had been called in advance. They came in with their guns on their belts and picked this patient up to carry him to isolation. He fought the assault. As illegal as this was, resisting in a psych unit only gets one in trouble. The nurses hid in their station behind enclosed glass. The rest of us were nearby in the line of whatever might break out. I was appalled that isolation and restraints were used on this patient for punishment, NOT safety. I was shocked at the wimpiness of the nurses who did nothing to protect us from having to watch this scene. I did report this to Dr. Noonan after my discharge, but apparently, he now had become one of *them*.

After a technician refused to let me take a shower without his supervision, I took one anyway without a towel and put my dirty scrubs back on without drying off. I had heard that this hospital had a couple of attempted hangings on their shower heads that were supposed to break off with body weight to prevent suicide. The shower head did not break away and a couple of people, two in a year, had succeeded in completing a suicide while on this unit. That is why patients were no longer allowed to take showers without supervision. Why didn't they fix the architecture after the first event? This was inexcusable. I would even go as far to say that they were responsible for at least the second sentinel event. I hoped that they had been sued, but I never actually heard about it.

When I asked the tech for my eyebrow pencil, a simple crayon that would have been allowed in my place of work, he said he did not have time to supervise me using it. I told him I needed my eyebrows before I would leave the unit for dinner (this place had a dining hall). I then noticed that "escape precautions" had been added to the board. If I had not become so angry and humiliated, I might have been able to see the humor in all of the ridiculousness of it.

Now this was the last straw. This girl from the south, in spite of her southern lady like manners, was going ballistic with anger. Of course, anger in a psych unit earns one a whole lot of diagnoses. I was afraid of this place. I signed myself out. I was not on a hold and they could not legally hold me. An female staff psychiatrist tried to talk me out of it. I insisted. I was not unsafe and I told her that this place was a disgrace to the profession. Without safety issues, they could not keep me. I signed out against medical advice.

The next day, I quit my job at Memorial and never went back after going on leave. I could take no more. All of psychiatry, *in all* of its forms, simply had been one big mess up, at least in my life. I saw Dr. Noonan only one or two times after that. I lost my temper badly in front of him. I do not think that I had ever yelled at anyone like that. It had been building up in me for a very long time. That hospital should have had its doors closed by the state. I would have sued, but psychiatric patients generally do not have any credibility in court. I could not be made out to be crazy in a court room. Dr. Noonan admitted that he had other patients who reported traumatic stress after being held there. I guess my biggest disappointment was the only good guy I had worked with had sold his soul out by taking part of it all. How could he care so little about me to place protocols over the emotional welfare of his patient. He had to have been insightful enough to have known the affect it would have on me. We said our goodbyes shortly after and I made sure that the ending was pleasant.

I wrote a letter to the director of the hospital. I wrote a letter to the CEO of the parent hospital in the same town. I wrote to the State Division of Mental Health. Of course, I received no response. Like I said, psych patients have no credibility. How could all of this happen? It was easy to see how normal inside I was, yet could see myself from a clinical eye and see how crazy I looked. Once the Psychiatric Train leaves the station, one just is not allowed to get off. It simply becomes a runaway. I flushed all of my medications and went off all of them cold turkey after being medication unnecessarily for twenty five years. This would prove to be a mistake. The withdrawals were terrible. They had told me that these substances were not addictive. They are in fact addictive, but in a different presentation than a drug of abuse. The withdrawal needs to be done slowly, but I had not yet learned this. It would be next to impossible to find a doctor who would support one in getting off the medications. I had to do it by myself.

I had nightmares for about a year after my hospital experience. I dreamed that I *really was* going crazy and was losing control of myself in public places. I dreamed of being locked up in places and trying to escape. I dreamed that the police were chasing me to have me committed somewhere. These dreams are typical of a post traumatic experience. Dreams are rarely repeats of the actual event, but rather "variations on a theme" in presentation.

The withdrawals were horrible. I had been on multiple medications, especially antidepressants for over twenty one years at this point. At the time I stopped taking them, I had been on four antidepressants, had a new anticonvulsant for that infamous euphoria that I had never had, anti-anxiety medications, and had also just come off some pain pills after the surgery. I never had a problem with pain pills. I had only had them after surgeries, but this probably compounded the problem. Looking back on it, I now believe that two changes in my medications probably pushed me over the edge into a state of restlessness and akisthesia that made it easy for any stressor to cause me to do something impulsive.

Akisthesia is a known phenomenon that I never actually saw diagnosed or recognized on the units. A sudden drug change can induce it, especially certain categories. Psychiatric nurses are all trained in the possibility of this occurrence in our patients. Going on certain drugs can induce it. My abrupt termination of one antidepressant, the only constant drug that was part of my medication regime the whole twenty one years, had been stopped abruptly prior to my impulsive act. I also had a couple of new ones on board. I was trying to be better. I had researched the drug Trazadone a few weeks before and discovered that reports had been made that reported that it could turn and actually increase symptoms of depression. When I stopped it, I was unable to sleep at all. That was part of the withdrawal symptoms. I became restless for several days with an inability to stay still. I had paced around the house for hours for several days and nights. When I got home from the hospital, I cried for hours and days. I wondered how many times had we missed this in the hospital. We always thought the restless hall walkers were simply anxious or manic. How many times, was one suffering with the deepest of inner turmoil, so dark, so untouchable and unobservable by others? This level of suffering can be lethal. It is a misery that simply *cannot* be spoken. How many have taken their own lives while in this state because the pain is unbearable? How many times does that event illicit anger and blame, instead of compassion for suffering? If I had to imagine how miserable, dark, and awful Hell would be, I could never have imagined the deep, dark, inner turmoil of akisthesia.

Determined to stay off the drugs, I took a trip to the Caribbean island of St. Martin. A good friend had sold me her time share and I had a luxury resort for a whole week for only a few hundred dollars. When I got there, I was having tremors all over my body from the withdrawal. My anxiety was high and I could not sleep. I feared that I would die of withdrawal in the tropics and I would never be found. I left after only two days because I was afraid I would not make it home.

Upon returning home, I was determined to find another way. In the throes of withdrawals, I started to research treatment alternatives. I was still grieving my father's death and was in no shape to return to work, nonetheless, psychiatric nursing. I discovered a book by Dr. Peter Breggin called <u>Your Drug May Be Your Problem</u>. The book explained everything. The side effects to all of the medications I had taken for over twenty years were explained. The withdrawal had symptoms and I was experiencing them all.

Chapter 12

County Mental Health Center

I needed to get the disability system off my back because they required that I be in treatment. I was done being in treatment. I had to go back to work. I was disappointed that my resignation from my job did not get me off the system from my employer. They kept sending me checks. I had no skills in nursing outside of psychiatry. I could have used more time off to redirect my work life, but necessity for income took precedence over any new career plans. I would not comply with any more psychiatric treatment. At this time, it was clear that I was a normal person, but I had not yet learned that perhaps most, or at least many, people on medications did not need them as well. At this time, the United States had entered a difficult economic recession. It was not a good time to be out of work. Even registered nurses were being laid off in my community. I accepted a job that I did not really want as medication nurse at the County Mental Health center. Because they remembered me during my rehabilitation counseling years, I was easily hired. I was now free of all medications and was feeling quite well. I could not get a job in a medical setting because my medical skills were rusty.

This job would prove to be the easiest job I had ever had. At the same time, it turned out to be the job I would end up hating the most. My position was all about medications. My job was to call in medication refills. Medical records needed to be checked prior to refilling the medications. Because the job was not full time, I was also hired to work on an "as needed basis" in their residential treatment center, an unlocked unit that was considered to be semi hospitalization. The employees at County Mental Health were extremely nice people, wanting to help those in need with only sincere desire to be of benefit to others. Their intentions were admirable. Their methods, however, were now misguided by public health insurance agencies that required a diagnosis to receive treatment.

I became uncomfortable right away. There were people still working in the center who had worked there ten years before that knew me as a "consumer" of mental health services. I went out of my way to avoid contact with these individuals as I attempted to just be an employee that did not have a disability. I became concerned that it had now been a decade since I shared clients from the center with rehabilitation services and my former clients were still receiving services there. The names of my former clients were on some of the refills that I had to call in. Occasionally, I would hear the names on the message system that needed a certain medication called in. I was surprised that some of them were still on the medications because they were not deemed to be actually mentally ill when I served them. The clients that I recognized were more chaotic in their lives than when I worked with them. They were observed to be on more medications than the decade before. Diagnoses had been bumped up to more severe levels of chronicity. Some whom had taken only an antidepressant, were now labeled with more severe chronic mental illness and were on heavy doses of the "newer generation" of antipsychotic medications. Most were now in the system as social security disability patients and were not well enough to work.

I knew the psychiatrist who managed the pediatric patients. She had been the medical director of the psychiatric unit at Memorial several years before. She had more medications to refill than all of the other doctors combined. She was prescribing rather hefty doses of heavy antipsychotic medications to small children as young as three or four years of age. I had to wonder how such a young child could possibly present to require that much. *How bad does a toddler have to be to make a doctor prescribe powerful antipsychotics?* These young children were often on antidepressants as well. Their little brains were not even fully developed yet and I wondered if these drugs could be harmful. I knew of no studies or FDA approval to prescribe these drugs to small children. Unsearched and "off label" uses of psychotropic drugs had become common place in psychiatry. Medication protocols are set in stone before any true drug approval was ever legally given in some cases.

The indigent population was commonplace in community services. It is easy to speculate how some of these children had fallen into the" psych trap". If an altercation occurred in the home, the police often got involved. In cases of domestic discord, parents and the children as well were often sentenced by the court system to participate in community mental health services. Often these individuals were given diagnoses for behaviors only, and were court ordered to comply. Some of these parents had no choice about whether they or their children would receive treatment. This population often did not even appear to be ill when they came to the center. Bad parenting, domestic altercations, and angry behaviors were deemed to be symptoms of a mental illness. Better coping skills were not taught as far as I was able to observe. When the legal system is involved, the parents had no choice about their care or they were in danger of losing custody of their children by Social Services. This kind of action is sometimes appropriate, but all too often, a simple incident started the process. I agreed with the process of rescuing an abused child, but all too often this was not the case at all. I also learned that foster parents in my state were paid more if the foster child was on a psychotropic medication. There was thus, little or no incentive or encouragement to get the children off the medications. Being indigent in our society places a target on their backs for involuntary interventions.

The indigent population also provide a huge profit for the pharmaceutical industry. Their Medicaid insurance would pay the high prices of new brand name medications. My insurance company would only pay for the generic version of a drug if it was available. With Medicaid in my state, the higher prices were covered. This allowed the physician to prescribe the newest designer drug available. The pharmaceutical representatives would provide many free samples for the indigent patient. The samples saved money for the center for those who were without any kind of insurance. This was an effective marketing strategy to get the doctors to prescribe a drug when it was started without cost. Sometime, later, the patient would be placed on the Medicaid system, so the drugs were continued because they were covered with very high costs to the taxpayer who could not access them.

The physicians at County were too busy to meet with the many pharmaceutical sales representatives that visited us daily without appointments. The medication nurse was responsible for these interactions. They would provide us with many free samples of everything that was still being sold under a brand name. One afternoon a sales representative informed me that he would no longer be providing us with samples of the drug called Risperdal. He informed me that the drug was going to be generic soon and therefore we needed to switch all of our patients on Risperdal to the new and improved product called Invega. He went on to inform me that Invega was the new and improved Risperdal. I inquired how Invega differed from Risperdal. He informed me that the pharmaceutical company had changed "a molecule" to make it new and improved. I politely reminded the representative that it is hard for our patients to change their medications, a process that comes with some risks to patients. He stated that they will be better stabilized with the new version. Just as the cost of a medication became affordable for the indigent patient and the tax payer who funds public systems, they were kept on brand name medications that I suspected were not significantly different. I did not trust any pharmaceutical representative after that.

One of the striking situations at County was the recent acknowledgment that the center rarely discharged a patient. Many patients had been clients of the center for decades. Meetings were taking place monthly of all medical staff to discuss how the center could begin discharging patients due to funding shortages. I was concerned that before that time, the center never even entertained discharging clients. It appeared that their clients were considered chronic and getting well was not on the agenda. Virtually all clients were considered biologically ill and incapable of full recovery. This was appalling to me that virtually all clients were being placed in a diagnostic box that had no exit at all. I never saw any treatment plans that included plans to wean patients off their medications. This was a disgrace in my eyes. I had already proven that at least in *my* case, one could get well. I took absolutely no medications of any kind at that point. My situation simply could not be that unusual. It was assumed from the beginning of treatment that the majority were going to be forever ill. This was such a sad thought to me that I began to wonder if anyone really benefited from public mental health services at all. It appeared to me that a progression of mild symptoms to severe symptoms was the course of events if one was to receive mental health treatment with medications. The efficacy of any mental health treatment was beginning to look quite dubious to me.

The few shifts I worked in the residential treatment center took me back to a place too close to my previous work in the inpatient setting. Psychotherapists, two year master degreed professionals, were in charge of all of the therapy that took place. I was always aware that one did not need a bachelor's degree in psychology to qualify to be in a master degree psychology program. Some of these professionals had undergraduate degrees in unrelated fields that contributed nothing to their expertise. Though some of these therapists are very good at what they do, they are not medical professionals. Yet they are allowed to diagnose the most severe of conditions. Most had only two years of training. The psychiatrist had little hands on involvement beyond the prescribing of medications. Change of shift report was intolerable to me as I found myself squirming in my seat listening to these "wannabe" shrinks go on endlessly with their psychobabble with the use of Freudian terms that I had not heard since my own psychoanalysis, now twenty years in the past. They discussed unresolved Oedipal complexes and "unconscious" behaviors with their own perceptions of what may be going on in someone's head. By now, this kind of talk sounded like nonsense to me, never getting to the root of ones suffering and pain caused by real life events. Coping skills for all of life's normal challenges were not discussed.

Because there are *no* objective tests to confirm *any* diagnosis, I found it hard to believe that at least sometimes, there would be an exception to the rule. It would not be long before I realized that there was no longer a place for me as a psychiatric nurse in any setting. I still believed in healing.

Chapter 13

A New Career Path

I refinanced my house and used the money to take a clinical refresher course to redirect my nursing into another area. I did well in the class. My old clinical skills came back quickly. I learned to start IVs again and refreshed my skills in wound care. I spent the next eighteen months reshaping my skills. In the end, I could not return to clinical nursing. My congenital kneecap deformity was progressing me toward total knee replacements and I just could not work on my feet anymore.

While I was attempting to experiment in other medical fields, I worked a number of per diem shifts in nursing homes in the three towns near my home. I took a night shift at a rather nice one shortly after finishing my refresher course. I took the night shift often, thinking that they would be easier while I refreshed my skill. As I entered one night at change of shift, I was given report on a patient whose name sounded familiar. I repeated his name to myself and stared to the evening shift nurse that the name was familiar. Knowing I had worked in psychiatry, she stated that I had probably encountered him somewhere because he had been "around the system". She said, "He is the one with schizophrenia". I looked in on him while he was sleeping. There I saw Kevin, my former rehabilitation client, now approaching the age of 60, A decade had passed since I had seen him at Middleton when I learned he had been diagnosed with manic depression and had been brain damaged by his electroshock treatment. Now, he was labeled with a more severe psychotic disorder. "How could this be?" I could see his path so clearly. He came to me for arthritis, I offered him treatment and helped him get on antidepressant medications to help him deal with painful memories of his mother's suicide. I had done enough research by this time to realize that I had started him on his path of destruction. His first antidepressant had side effects that labeled him with bipolar disorder. He then received neuroleptic medication that made him look the part, and then he progressed to schizophrenia. On top of it all, antipsychotic medications are known to cause diabetes and he had developed this as well. It was clear, I had played a part in his iatrogenic symptoms and he was in a nursing home at the age of 60. As I awoke him at 5 am to check his blood sugar, he looked at me with a puzzled expression. This time, I did not identify myself. I finished my shift and went home and cried for hours. I thought I was helping at the time. I wondered how many people had I unknowingly harmed. I would never administer a psychiatric medicine again.

My last stop in the nursing field was in nurse case management for a worker's compensation insurance company. I would be managing the medical data and approve procedures for people who had been injured on the job. I thought that broken bones and accidents was something I could do and care about. I would have no direct contact with my patients. My job was computer based. I would be off my painful knees. Even here, I ran into conflicts.

I became aware that psychiatric medications had infiltrated virtually every field of medicine. Some of my patients had been severely injured. I worked with the roofers and the construction workers who lost limbs, broke their backs, and sometimes had head injuries beyond repair. Yet, psychiatric medications were being given to them as well. When too many pain medicines were taken, the patient had a tendency to be depressed. Then an antidepressant medication was added. Of course, these rarely worked on this population, and then a neuroleptic medication would be added to enhance its effect. The side effects would then begin to present a psychiatric picture and before it was all over, they had psychiatric diagnoses of their own. In fact, during this job, I attended three trainings on chronic pain issues. All three presentations concluded that all pain patients were actually personality disordered and had some kind of psychiatric diagnosis. A construction worker who was completely normal before he fell off a roof, would become a psychiatric patient with just as many diagnoses as the psychiatric patients in my hospital. If our society wants to give medications for thoughts, feelings and behaviors, why is it so hard to believe that the side effects to these substances would be manifested with *thoughts, feelings, and behaviors*? In my opinion, it is not even logical.

Antidepressants are now given for smoking cessation, weight loss, anxiety, insomnia, and chronic pain. My observation was that the majority of people diagnosed with manic depression have been on antidepressant medications prior to the presentation to any such symptoms. As I have mentioned earlier in this writing, they often cause agitated side effects. This was used as a diagnostic criteria for this alleged diagnosis. I have to ask, that if one does not present as manic depressive before taking antidepressants, why are they continued? There would be no such diagnosis if they simply did not take the drug. Instead, it is viewed as evidence that there must be a severe and organic mental illness, not yet erupted, that had to be managed with further medications. I now believe that most so called "organic mental illnesses" are created, not born, *at least in many cases*. There is still no evidence of any genetic illness at this time. It is only theory. Yes, occasionally we see this diagnosed in several members of the same family. We assume that we inherit it. We do not want to consider that perhaps nutritional habits, coping skills, and unhealthy lifestyles are inherited as well as they are set by example. It remains a puzzle. One of the disturbing things is that the textbook definition of such a syndrome includes illogical states of euphoria. I have rarely seen anything like that, and some who are diagnosed with other labels have displayed this as well. The most common symptom that leads one to the diagnosis is anger. We live in a frustrated world. Anger was never a disease before the invention of antidepressant medications and the authorship of the Diagnostic Statistical Manual, a book that places a diagnosis to **fill in the blank** on the insurance form.

There is no question that people get psychotic, depressed, confused, etc. The reason for it is unclear. I remember a weekend on the unit when there were four psychotic patients hospitalized. They all looked similar in presentation. All were admitted on the evening shift, so the "on call" psychiatrist gave them "psychotic disorder" as their admission diagnosis, sight unseen. By the time they were discharged, one was known to have had altered mental status secondary to the steroids she had taken for her arthritis. One had an electrolyte imbalance. One had been abusing cocaine, and only one had a prior history of any psychiatric diagnosis. There is still so much we do not know. One thing is clear. Things are often not what they may appear to be. The good news that weekend was that the psychiatrist on call knew the differences. If our infamous Dr. Colley had been on duty, they would have all gone home on his favorite antipsychotic medication that gave to practically every patient. He gave it to everyone for everything, including a friend of mine who was referred to him for being sorrowful about being in hospice. He was dying. Giving a dying man an antipsychotic medication is perhaps the most useless reason for a prescription I ever heard of.

Chapter 14

Then Came Joe

Shortly after I resigned from the hospital, I was determined to find another way to heal from what was now, decades of discomforts. I called a former colleague, now in his own business as an acupuncturist, for suggestions to try a more natural and holistic approach to recovering from all of the damage the drugs had done to my psyche and body. I was under a great deal of stress with unemployment, drug withdrawal, and being a caregiver to my mother. I had read about a study that showed improvement with acupuncture in depressed patients.

"Joe, this is Toni", I said on the phone." I would like to try acupuncture for my depression". He had known of it because he had worked in the hospital at the time I went on leave. I told him that he could give me a referral if he felt that he knew me too well, but stated that he was perfectly comfortable in seeing me. He actually knew very little about what I had been through, and I had no plans of telling him anymore than what I thought he knew. On my first appointment, I disclosed that I was recently off of antidepressant medications for the first time in over twenty years. Instead of the usual lecture that we psych professionals gave about compliance, he surprised me. He said "congratulations"! He then said "Buddha says we all get to heal and be well". *What? I thought. Nobody ever told me I could be well.* I had become a chronic crazy person that needed to be managed, not healed. I knew I was for *once*, in the right place. He explained that acupuncture was about tapping into energetic healing by opening up our energetic meridians. He also stated that it did not matter if the patient believes in why it works, because it simply works. I started seeing him weekly at first. I had not told him my whole story. Nobody at the hospital was informed of my mental illness diagnosis. I certainly had not told anyone the story of my awful psychoanalysis. It took me months to get my story out to him as it seemed clear to me that he needed to know that I was actually coming off of many medications. It took us several years to get my whole story out again. Joe was not a psychotherapist. Even he was never informed of every detail of my life experience. It was not necessary in this kind of healing. We only talked a little bit before I would have treatment with his painless needles while relaxing to soft music. I was never going to tell him about my psychoanalysis and diagnosis, but over time, it all came out. He believed that everyone could heal from most anything. I wanted to go with that.

Acupuncture treatments had an amazing calming effect on me that would last for days. But the withdrawals of mood swings continued for quite some time and my insomnia reached new and unbearable heights. The acupuncture could not tackle all of it at once. I had arthritis in places and my painful back and knees benefitted from it as well. Because of that, absolutely everything spilled out for him to see. He never gave direct advice or formal counseling. But he also had psychiatric experience and seem to understand in a way that over a dozen doctors had not. The main thing he gave me was hope that everyone *really could* heal. He was an empathic man who always seemed to understand what others could not. He was patient and never was critical of what I was feeling. He would tell me that *any* feeling was OK. I felt that I could trust him.

Before it was all done and said I had to go off and on antidepressants again to eventually get over them. Having vowed to never see a shrink again, I ordered them from foreign pharmacies and continued to attempt to wean myself off more slowly. It would take five years and three attempts before I was done with it for good. I do not recommend this method or the purchase from foreign pharmacies to anyone. We need more physicians and practitioners who take the trouble to think "outside the box and educate themselves" with research, not just memorizing insurance protocols. We need practitioners who are empathic and who believe that people can get well. They need to meet people in the place where they *are*. At the same time, they need to have the courage to make their *own* assessments and not simply treat what another practitioner may have diagnosed.

I learned from our brief discussions before treatment that healing from trauma is about letting it all go by detaching from the past. We cannot change the past, so we cannot fix it. I had made the mistake of trying to get doctors to undo the damage that the first one had done. It was simply impossible. We cannot change that which never should have happened in the first place. We cannot ever forget the traumas of our past, but we can learn to not live there.

The most important thing that I learned from this very spiritually minded man was the belief in healing. He never tried to give me his spiritual beliefs. I sensed that he simply lived them and I could see that he had a peaceful way of being. He became a teacher in many ways by the example he demonstrated and by giving me permission to feel any way I wanted without pathologizing my feelings. I became more connected to my own experience of God, which ultimately made the difference. Love and empathy was my cure. I had become reconnected to the God in me on a whole new level. Joe was not afraid to be my friend. Joe also believed in fixing the physical self as well. I would change my diet to fresh foods only. I started eating more fruits and vegetables to cleanse my body and detoxify all of those medications that were stored in my fat cells. I began to exercise with swimming. All of these coping skills and lifestyle changes were given to me by Joe.

After my mother passed away, I left my job because I felt compromised with my integrity. I could not keep watching the making of a psychiatric patient because a normal construction worker had fallen off a roof.

By now I was old enough to tap into some retirement funds and I gave myself a break. No more psychotropic medications would ever be in my life. I grieved my mother, but did not crater. I did not resort back to psychotropic medications. My tumultuous childhood always complicated my diagnostic picture. She was almost ninety and her death seemed timely. I attempted to start my own business at home, but was unsuccessful in doing so. I lacked the capital and the skills to make anything work. I also continued to be unable to move on while I was still keeping secrets from my former colleagues who were my friends. My medical records were contaminated by false diagnoses and it seemed like I would never be free from my past. I quit doing routine medical care several years earlier. The medical system had traumatized me so severely, that I could not even see a dentist without fear and triggering my memories. As I began to feel better, others in my life did not understand why I had changed. They were still unaware of the details of my life. As we heal and change, so does everything else. If a relationship cannot handle the changes, we must move on. My closest friend in the world wanted nothing to do with me when I told her I had gotten well. I realize now, that it probably made her uncomfortable because she was travelling on the psychiatric freight train with her children. The only diagnosis that I deserved was Post Traumatic Stress secondary to all things related to psychiatry. Ultimately, even that would improve. I sold my house, left treasured friends behind, and moved to Mexico. I needed a place where there would be no past. I would never speak of it there.

Epilogue

My Paradise

It did not take me long to fall in love with my new home. A circle of friends developed quickly. I am known as a happy person. I have made friends with Mexicans and Gringos from all parts of the world. I have even dated. The culture is polite and kind. Public politeness is protocol and expected. I have seen no rudeness or public outbursts of anger. I see lovely Mexican parents gently guide their children without ever showing any frustration. They are happy hearted people. The poverty here can be striking to witness. At the same time, the sense of family and politeness can only breed a loving culture. The people of my small village lack the resources to go to a psychiatrist and pay for expensive designer medications. As a nurse, I always noticed that my Hispanic patients always had more visitors than other populations. When life throws them a hardship, they simply support and love each other through it. Perhaps my country could learn something from these kind and empathic people.

I notice everything like I never have before. Several times a week, I dress early and walk to the plaza of my village. I notice the green foliage and the beautiful flowers that bloom all year round. I sit in the shade and enjoy homemade treats from the local people who are earning a few extra pesos. I notice the colorful birds and there is always music coming from somewhere. It is like waking up from a thirty year coma and seeing the world for the first time. I even entrusted the Mexican medical system and found expert, compassionate, and affordable care. I had my knee replacement surgery and all went well. My surgical clearance exam was very thorough and I was told that I was normal and in good health. I would rather be told that I am *normal* than be told that I was the most beautiful woman in the world.

I can see that my soul could never have been injured. The soul is perfect. We were created that way. Now I can see it in myself. I will never see Joe again because I will not be returning to that state. I will be forever grateful to him for opening the door that others had locked.

Even still, I do carry a bit of sadness in my heart. Sometimes I let it out and let myself feel it. I cry a little and put it all back inside. It is simple grief, but it no longer dominates my life. I grieve for the innocence that was violated, my young adulthood and middle years that were sabotaged for chances of love and children, and for the emotional bluntness that I lived with for years that took away my music. I never became the expert musician that I wanted to be. I grieve for the financial devastation caused by futile care that will follow me through the rest of my days. It is alright, though. I am grateful for what I *do* have, for what I have learned, for healing, for peace, for surviving, and for giving myself the opportunity to learn joy.

My Mexican neighbors are getting used to my gringo presence. A few mothers trust me enough to let me play with their children a little. That makes me smile the rest of the day.

Commentary

I have no comment on the value of psychoanalysis as a therapeutic method. What is clear, is that *my* doctor did it very badly by inserting *his* own ego into *my* process. If an erotic transference appears in the process, it is the patient that takes the lead, not the doctor. Talking methods of psychotherapy can be life changing and transformational if handled with compassion, empathy, and skill. It can be devastating if the therapist is unskilled or has a personal need to insert his own ego in the process.

Psychiatrists, psychologists, and therapists deserve to be paid for their services. The field dramatically changed when health insurance began covering mental health services because a diagnosis is required for reimbursement. Psychiatry's attempt to be legitimized as a medical science has led to the creation of many labels and diagnoses to qualify for insurance reimbursement. As I look back on my thirty nine years in the healthcare arena, I have to note that at least ninety percent of the time, there is no effort to consider a patient well and healed in the mental health area. When a medication is prescribed, there is rarely a plan in place to wean the patient off the medications. Because mental health practitioners need to be paid for their services, there must be an assumption that the condition is caused by a physical illness. We still do not know if this is or not true. Regardless of the etiology of emotional distress, treatment must change toward getting better, healing, and most importantly, dealt with compassion and empathy. Insurance companies, as well as government are unenlightened to the Human Experience. It does not seem necessary in my eyes to pretend that matters of the heart are physical illnesses. Yet, at the same time, sometimes we need support and help to get through life's challenges, or we *will* become *physically* or emotionally ill.

Robert Whitaker cites in his book <u>Anatomy of an Epidemic</u> a study by the World Health Organization conducted in the late sixties, and then repeated ten years later compared individuals after a first psychotic episode treated with western medicine that provided follow up care with ongoing medications with third world countries where no long term care with medications was provided. It was found that ongoing medications in western medicine resulted in a 66 percent incidence of the patient becoming chronic with mental illness and permanent clients of a mental health system with ongoing medications. In the third world countries, the opposite was true. Sixty percent went back to their villages and lives and did not have a repeat occurrence. This population was not kept on psychotropic medications. Thirty three percent, or approximately one third in western civilizations did experience spontaneous recovery. In the third world countries, only one third became chronic.

We also know, through DNA testing that all of us have certain liver enzymes to metabolize medications. However, testing for personalization of medication is still not routine. Sometimes knowledge of the patient's enzymatic picture is key to medication success in areas even outside of psychiatry. Pain control and cancer treatment especially need personalization of medication choices. I have been tested and was told that I am one of the ten percent of Caucasians that have very little, or are slow metabolizers of the enzyme CPY2d6 which is responsible for many of the psychotropic medications I was prescribed. Of the thirty plus drugs that I was given, I know that at least 13 of them were medications that I could not even metabolize. This is some of the first objective evidence we have in choosing whether any medication is appropriate for an individual. Most of the many antidepressant drugs that I was given are metabolized by CYPD2d6 and explains, at least in part, the absurd and odd side effects I suffered.

Another issue of concern was discussed by Dr. Peter Breggin in his scientific paper: "Intoxication Anosognosia: The Spellbinding Effect of Psychiatric Drugs". He discusses clearly why so many people stay on their psychotropic medications despite uncomfortable side effects. This phenomenon has been clearly demonstrated to me by a number of personal acquaintances. A good friend of mine tried hard to convince me that he was better on his medications because he had become somewhat functional after a devastating divorce that triggered his depression. However, his stress levels only allowed him to work part time, his home was that of a hoarder and he remained acutely wounded by a divorce that was thirty years in the rears. He recently died in his sleep after to going to bed after taking a cocktail of psychotropic medications with alcohol. Another friend of mine believes in her antidepressant because she feels better for a few weeks after she starts it, then stops it only to start it again at a later time when her symptoms worsen from withdrawal from the drug. Antidepressant and neuroleptic medications were never designed for PRN use.

She cannot see that she is worsening her depression by going on and off her medication. Another example might be the depressed person who is aware that he or she feels a little better on the medication, but is unaware that weight gain, lethargy, loss of libido and increased blood glucoses are side effects of his or her medication. As a nurse, I have found it futile to even try to educate these people. They are unable to see through the mindspell of their medication and that their overall health is being compromised.

Too many medical protocols are based on correlation studies that have no proven tangible or objective evidence of causation. This is occurring in non-psychiatric arenas as well. Even the original Prozac research is dubious at best. It is similar to saying that eating too many tomatoes will kill you because most people who have died had eaten tomatoes. A high correlation is only a place to start exploring. All of us who have studied statistics know that correlation does not demonstrate causation by itself. A hypothesis must be proven. There is no excuse for us to be so uninformed in this age of the internet. I tell people that they should at least pay attention to their television sets when an ad is on for a psychotropic medication. Ignore the animations and listen to what they are saying when the volume decreases: they are telling the truth because they have to. Why isn't anyone listening?

References

1. <u>Anatomy of an Epidemic: Magic Bullets, Psychiatric Drugs and the Astonishingly Rise of Mental</u> <u>Illness in America</u>, Robert Whitaker
2. <u>Your Drug May Be Your Problem, How and Why to Stop Taking Psychiatric Medication,</u> Dr. Peter Breggin, MD
3. <u>Prozac Backlash</u>, Joseph Glenmullen MD
4. <u>The Antidepressant Handbook,</u> Peter Breggin MD
5. <u>Pharmacy Times, Get to Know an Enzyme: CPYD26.</u> John R Horn, PharmD.FCCP, and Philip D Hansten, Pharmd, published online: Tuesday, July 1 2008
6. **Scientfic paper by Dr. Peter Breggin:** <u>"Intoxication Anosognosia: The Spellbinding Effect of</u> <u>Psychiatric Drugs</u>", *Ethical Human Psychology and Psychiatry*, 8, 201-215, 2006.
7. <u>Physician's Desk Reference,</u>2014 edition (published annually)

Recommended Reading and Viewing in Addition to the above:

1. <u>The Antidepressant Solution: A Step by Step Guide to Safely Overcoming Antidepressant</u> <u>Withdrawal, Dependence, and Addiction</u>, Joseph Glenmullen MD
2. <u>Toxic Psychiatry</u>, Peter Breggin MD
3. <u>Psychiatric Drug Withdrawal: A Guide for Prescribers, Therapists, Patients and their Families,</u> Peter Breggin MD 2012
4. <u>My Lobotomy</u>, Howard Duffy, Random House, 2007
5. <u>www.cchr.org</u> videos: The Marketing of Madness, The Diagnostical and Statistical Manual, Prescription for Violence.

Made in the USA
Middletown, DE
13 November 2017